The Kite Route

THE Kite Route

Story of the Denver & Interurban Railroad

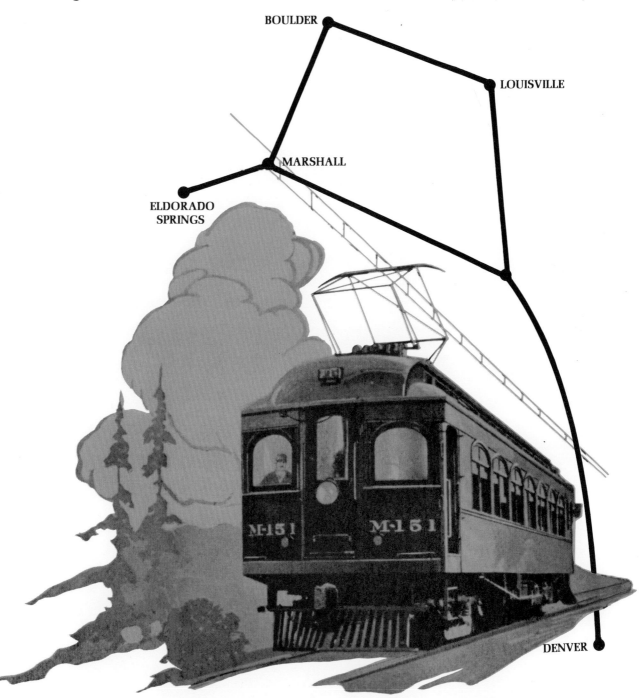

William C. Jones & Noel T. Holley

PRUETT **P** *PUBLISHING COMPANY*
Boulder, Colorado

The following abbreviations have been used for photo credits.

CHS—Colorado Historical Society
CLB—Carnegie Branch Library for Local History, Boulder
CRRM—Colorado Railroad Museum
DPL—Denver Public Library, Western History Department
NRHS—National Railway Historical Society
UCWH—University of Colorado, Western Historical Collections

Library of Congress Cataloging-in-Publication Data

Jones, William C., 1937-
   The kite route.

   Bibliography: p.
   Includes index.
   1. Denver & Interurban Railroad—History. I. Holley, Noel T.
1947-   . II. Title.
HE2791.D383J66   1986   385'.5   86-25190
ISBN 0-87108-721-9

First Edition

1 2 3 4 5 6 7 8 9

Printed in the United States of America.

Endpapers: On April 2, 1909 L.C. McClure captured forever this superb scene as M-152 passed Standley Lake en route to Denver.—*DPL*

Jacket and Title Page: D & I advertising folder.—*A.A. Paddock Collection*

Half Title Page: A head-on view of M-157 as it pauses at Louisville during an inspection trip when the line opened.—*Edmunds Collection*

Editor's Comment

The *Kite Route* is in reality two books in one. Quite unknown to each other, co-authors Noel Holley and William Jones both had a long-standing interest in the Denver & Interurban Railroad. In this volume their separate endeavors were brought together.

Holley had begun researching the D & I some years ago after building an HO scale model of an interurban for the Denver HO Club's extensive layout at the Colorado Railroad Museum. His interest led to the eventual publication of a feature on the D & I in the *Bulletin* of the National Model Railroad Association. While living in Denver, Holley continued to research details in the line's history at the Federal Records Center, State Historical Society and Colorado Railroad Museum, but his move from the Denver area prevented his acquiring a collection of photos of the D & I, and he eventually became involved in other publishing projects.

Jones co-authored *Mile-High Trolleys*, a history of the Denver Tramway, in 1965 and was keenly interested in the Denver & Interurban. In discussing future book ideas with the staff of Pruett Publishing the D & I was considered and the idea met with favor. It is interesting to note that the interurban once passed in front of the Pruett offices. Jones learned of Holley's work on the D & I after reading his NMRA article and invited him to participate in a D & I history; the two agreed to combine efforts. Jones devoted two years to collecting photographs of the long gone interurban, locating maps, folders and other material to illustrate Holley's text. The result is this book.

Just half a century ago the D & I was abandoned. Today the Denver-Boulder corridor is daily congested with automobile traffic. With no prospects for improvement in sight one must wonder when we will progress back to the days of high speed, non-polluting, electric interurban rail passenger service on the Kite Route.

Acknowledgements

Many individuals and institutions provided materials and information during preparation of *The Kite Route*. Among the institutions were the Carnegie Branch Library for Local History in Boulder, the Colorado Historical Society, Public Service Company of Colorado, the Intermountain Chapter of the National Railway Historical Society, and the University of Colorado Western Historical Collections. Robert W. Richardson, curator of the Colorado Railroad Museum and Augie Mastrogiuseppe, curator of photographs at the Western History Department of the Denver Public Library, provided a wealth of information and photos from these institutions.

Morris Cafky and Ed Haley shared their memories of riding the D & I for the enjoyment of future readers. Haley's considerable assistance in locating and identifying photos was invaluable.

Important help was given by Charles Albi, Matilda Campbell, Kenton Forrest, Dick Kindig, Al Kilminster, Gene McKeever, Laurence Paddock, Don Robinson and Martha Sherriff.

F. Hol Wagner generously allowed the use of his fine D & I equipment drawings and was helpful in locating photos and data.

Dorothy Michael, daughter of D & I General Manager William H. Edmunds, provided numerous photos from her father's collection and just as importantly, along with her son Roger, furnished a wealth of background on the D & I during a morning interview as they drew on their family memories.

The staff of Pruett Publishing Company provided their usual strong support for this project, a very necessary ingredient in production of a book.

Court House and Denver Interurban Car.
Boulder, Colo.

M-156 pauses on Pearl Street in front of the Boulder County Court House circa 1910. This colored post card was produced from a black and white photo to which color was added, a popular technique prior to full color photography. The small black marks near the upper left and right are from a postal cancelling machine.—*CRRM*

Table of Contents

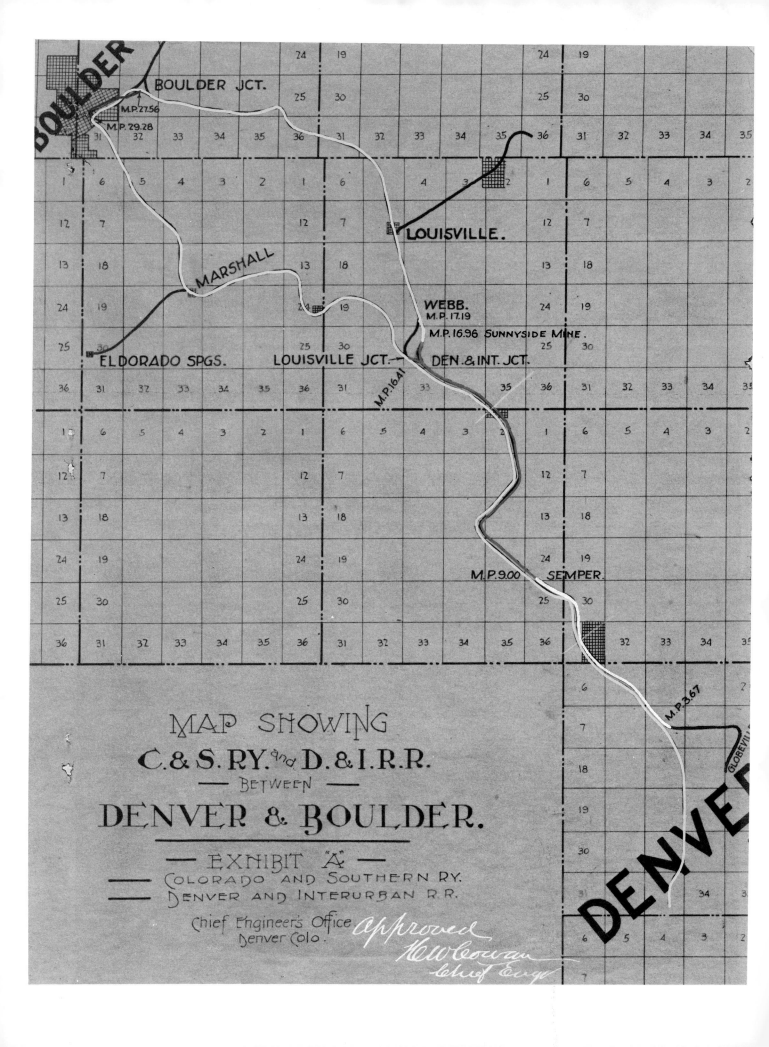

BOULDER

24 19   24 19

BOULDER JCT.

25 30   25 30

M.P. 27.56

M.P. 29.28

31 32 33 34 35 36 31 32 33 34 35 36 31 32 33 34 35

1 6 5 4 3 2 1 6 4 3 2 1 6 5 4 3 2

12 7 12 7 12 7

LOUISVILLE.

13 18 MARSHALL 13 18 13 18

24 19 24 19 WEBB. 24 19
M.P. 17.19

M.P. 16.96 Sunnyside Mine.

25 30 25 30 25 30

ELDORADO SPGS. LOUISVILLE JCT. DEN. & INT. JCT.

36 31 32 33 34 35 36 31 M.P.16.61 33 35 36 31 32 33 34 35

1 6 5 4 3 2 1 6 5 4 3 2 1 6 5 4 3 2

12 7 12 7 12 7

13 18 13 18 13 18

24 19 24 19 24 19

M.P. 9.00 SEMPER.

25 30 25 30 25 30

36 31 32 33 34 35 36 31 32 33 34 35 36 32 33 34 35

6 2

M.P. 3.67

7

GLOBEVILLE

DENVER

18

MAP SHOWING
C. & S. RY. and D. & I. R. R.
— BETWEEN —
DENVER & BOULDER.

— EXHIBIT "A" —

—— COLORADO AND SOUTHERN RY.
—— DENVER AND INTERURBAN R. R.

Chief Engineer's Office
Denver Colo.

Approved
H.W.Cowan
Chief Eng.

19

30

31 34 3.

6 5 4 3 2

7

1

The Denver & Interurban Railroad Company
A Colorado & Southern Subsidiary

The Denver & Interurban Railroad Company was incorporated on September 10, 1904. It was a corporation wholly owned and controlled by the Colorado & Southern Railway. It was created to bring fast, efficient, electric local passenger service to the Colorado & Southern's route between Denver, Boulder and Fort Collins, and to extend electrified branches into the countryside around Fort Collins. The total electrified trackage was to be approximately 110 miles, which was most of the Colorado & Southern's Fort Collins District.

The impetus for these plans was the rapid population growth which Colorado was experiencing at the time. Although the entire state of Colorado contained only 419,000 residents in 1890, the population grew by 29 percent between 1890 and 1900. After the turn of the century, people were arriving at an even faster rate. The population grew by another forty-eight percent between 1900

and 1910. A large number of these people were making their homes in an area from Denver to Fort Collins. Their presence and the expected continuing high population growth represented a significant business opportunity for the Colorado & Southern Railway. Highways were poor and automobile ownership was low. People who wished to commute or ship products between towns did so by train. The C & S had a more direct route in this area than did its competitors, the Union Pacific and the Chicago, Burlington & Quincy. The C & S exploited this advantage and worked hard to increase the volume of the traffic, and revenues for both freight and passenger operations. It went so far as to offer economic incentives for the development of lineside industries. The intended key to increased passenger business was fast, frequent service, provided at a low cost by electric interurban cars.

t. No. ....   Treas. No. ....   Audit No. **350**

The Denver & Interurban Railroad Company.

rge .... To *C. G. Burgoyne* .... Dr.

               350   Of *New York, NY*

               Pay *Same*

th of *August* 190*7* Address *Cor. Walker & Centre Sts*

For *100 Temporary Gold Bonds*   *10 | 50*

Construction of the D & I was financed by sale of bonds to the C & S and in 1907
an order was placed for the printing of these bonds.—*Both, CRRM*

This photo was taken from the Argo smelter looking south at about Forty-seventh Avenue on February 16, 1906 with railroad cars at the smelter visible in the foreground. The D & I route via the Tramway's Globeville line would be built on Fox Street which runs from right of center off the right margin. The Burlington line which was electrified into Union Station crosses by the stack at right to the left center.—CHS

In 1904, the Colorado & Southern was a fast growing company, only five years old. It was incorporated in December 1898, and on January 11, 1899, it took over most of the properties of the bankrupt Denver, Leadville & Gunnison Railway and the Union Pacific, Denver and Gulf Railway. Both lines had been Union Pacific Railroad subsidiaries until they experienced financial problems and were sold under foreclosure.

In 1902, The Colorado & Southern began expanding its route and holdings, primarily through buying or building subsidiary lines in Colorado and Texas. The 1904 creation of the Denver & Interurban was one of these expansion moves.

Following its incorporation, the D & I directors and officers worked to inaugurate service within four years. On April 17, 1906, they secured entry into Denver via a contract with the Denver Tramway Company. On July 23, 1906, the D & I gained an entry into Fort Collins through a franchise for interurban and street railway service. On February 2, 1907, a contract was signed with the Northern Colorado Power Company for the delivery of electric power and the construction of a pole line with overhead trolley. A franchise to enter Boulder was granted on October 4, 1907. Tracks were laid or improved during 1907 and 1908, and a contract covering joint operation was signed with the Colorado & Southern in 1909. That agreement was back-dated to July 1, 1908. The Fort Collins Street Railway began running on January 1, 1908, and interurbans entered service on the line from

Denver to Boulder on June 23, 1908. The interurban cars never reached Fort Collins because that plan was vetoed by the Burlington Railroad. The Burlington purchased the Colorado & Southern in December 1908, as part of a program to link the Great Lakes and the Gulf Coast via Burlington rails. The Burlington did not favor steam railroad electrification, and had little interest in interurban lines. It moved to focus the energies of the C & S on larger goals. These were: a rail tie between the C & S at Fort Collins and a Burlington terminal in Cheyenne, Wyoming; an improved connection with the Fort Worth & Denver which was a C & S subsidiary in Texas; and, laying heavier rail throughout the C & S system. Since the Denver & Interurban never generated large profits, the plan to extend the electrification to Fort Collins never resurfaced.

As was typical for C & S subsidiaries, the D & I was incorporated as a separate entity from the C & S. Through interlocking directorships, the C & S was in a position to totally absorb subsidiaries if they were an overwhelming financial success. On the other hand, separate incorporation and financing assured that the C & S was not liable for the debts and obligations of subsidiaries which failed. There was an additional benefit that also resulted from this arrangement. Subsidiaries could act as an arm of the Colorado & Southern whenever this was advantageous, and they could also claim to be legally separate and independent if that better suited the corporate goals.

As officers of a separate and independent

corporation in the eyes of the law, the directors of the Denver & Interurban issued 1,015 shares of capital stock and sold $1,079,000 in mortgage bonds. These were used to finance construction and start up of the line. The Colorado & Southern bought all of the bonds when they were issued on the New York bond market by the Guaranty Trust Company of New York. The C & S also bought all but seven of the stock shares which were issued. The remaining shares were purchased by the seven members of the D & I Board of Directors. As members of the board changed from year to year, the stock was passed from old to new members. These seven men were typically high-level Colorado & Southern officials.

The interlocking management arrangement was further cememted by the fact that members of the D & I board additionally held the posts of president, vice-president, secretary-treasurer and general solicitor for the D & I.

The ties to the C & S resulted in an interurban company which was unusually strong in regards to management's ability to protect corporate interests. The terms of D & I agreements with other companies were generally quite favorable, and with the C & S they were "sweetheart deals." In addition, when the D & I went to court, public sentiment and naive local lawyers were no match for the C & S corporate strategists.

A train moves across the University of Colorado campus about 1890 on the line later electrified for the D & I. Below is a view of the little known coal mining community of Langford in the late 1890s. A short distance east of Marshall, this approximate location will later be known as Gorman.—*Both DPL*

In this 1900 view of Boulder the C & S line can be seen crossing Broadway after leaving the university campus and a short distance beyond crosses Marine Street as it curves toward downtown the depot. In a few years D & I interurbans will be following this route.—DPL

The Northern Colorado Power Company plant designed to serve the D & I is nearing completion in this construction photo at Lafayette on February 24, 1907.—Public Service Company of Colorado

The Denver & Interurban Railroad Company

Charge _____   To   Phillips Construction Co. & O'Gara,   Dr.

____ D.B.Const. _____   Of _____

____ 11. _____

                   Pay _____ Same.

Month of *April*   190 8   Address 50 Railroad Bldg., Denver, Colo.

For

        Rent of steam shovel during days shovel
was idle owing to track between Semper and
Louisville Jct., not being ready for ballast:

14 days @ $10.00 per day....................$140.00

Northern Colorado Power Company contracted to do all electrification work for the D & I with the C & S supplying two trains with railroad crews. This photo was taken from the roof of a car on a construction train early in 1908. At this time other work forces were laying new track and improving existing line for D & I operations as noted above in connection with laying ballast.— *Both, CRRM*

The wire trains had apparatus for stringing the wire from reels over rollers and up to the poles. A one-day record was set when 26 men on the two trains (including crews) installed wire on 117 poles over a length of seven miles.—*CRRM*

13

BEAUTIFUL BOULDER IS NOW WITHIN 55 MINUTES OF DENVER

Boulder is now a suburb of Denver. The opening of the Denver & Interurban electric line yesterday placed the beautiful town, which stands at the portal of the mountains, within fifty-five minutes' ride of this city. For a part of the thirty miles of country through which the new line passes the cars attain a speed in excess of a mile a minute. On the electric cars passengers are not annoyed with cinders, smoke or dust. This method of transportation gives more pleasure to travelers than any yet discovered.

TOOK SCORE OF GUESTS.

Officials of the Denver & Interurban Railway company, controlled by the Colorado & Southern railway, at 3 o'clock yesterday afternoon left the city with more than a score of guests for a trip of inspection over the new electric road. The run to Boulder was made in an hour and eleven minutes. When the regular schedule is established sixteen minutes will be cut off that time.

Among the guests on the trip was John F. Wallace, who for a year was in charge of the work of the Panama canal and who is president of the Electric Properties company, which is interested in the Northern Colorado Power company, which supplies power to the Denver & Interur-

ban. Eldorado Springs), University of Colorado and Boulder. Leaving Boulder, cars return by way of Louisville, passing through Inland, Culbertson, Weiserhorn, Burkes, Louisville and Webb.

For the present a motor car will operate between Marshall, on the main line, and Eldorado Springs. The Denver & Interurban has ordered twelve cars, and when they are all in use direct service from Denver to Eldorado Springs will be established.

CAR EVERY TWO HOURS.

The Denver terminus of the Denver & Interurban will for the present be at Sixteenth and Arapahoe streets. Cars will leave for Boulder every two hours.

Complete list of those who made up the official party yesterday follows: Governor Henry A. Buchtel, Mayor Robert W. Speer, William J. Barker, president of the North Colorado Power company; Frank W. Frueauff, vice president and general manager of the Denver Gas & Electric company; B. F. James, president of the Denver & Interurban railroad; Isaac T. Earl, mayor of Boulder; John F. Wallace, president of the Electric Properties company of New York; F. W. Mahl, general purchasing agent of the C. & S.; H. C. Van Buskirk, superintendent of motive power of the C. & S.; E.

C. & S.; J. H. Brandbury, general auditor of the C. & S.; C. F. Wolfer, C. & S. physician; J. L. Woods of Chicago, representing the Railway Steel Springs company; N. A. Carle of Westinghouse, Church, Kerr & Co.; Thomas C. Scott, traffic manager of the Colorado Manufacturers' association; L. M. Cargo, with Westinghouse, Church, Kerr & Co.; Charles B. Culbertson, vice president of the Colorado & Northwestern railroad; J. W. Baugher, superintendent of construction for Westinghouse, Church, Kerr & Co.; E. M. Burgess, general manager of the Colorado Telephone company; Lieutenant Governor E. R. Harper; George T. Headrick, Westinghouse agent; H. A. Rhodes, chief engineer of the Colorado Telephone company; J. C. Ferguson, general agent of the Union Pacific in Denver; J. A. Munroe, freight traffic manager of the Union Pacific at Omaha; W. G. Matthews, line superintendent for the Denver City Tramway company; A. W. Whitford, J. L. Henritzy, S. E. Leonard, Charles R. Brock, J. P. Hymer, William R. Rathvon, president of the Boulder Commercial association, E. L. Scholtz, president of the Denver chamber of commerce; J. B. Cox of Chicago, consulting engineer; A. B. Church, vice president and general manager of the Eldorado Springs Resort com-

PROMINENT CITIZENS WHO WERE THE GUESTS OF THE C. & S. YESTERDAY, STARTING ON THEIR TRIP OVER THE NEW INTERURBAN LINE TO BOULDER.

ban. Frank Frueauff, manager of the Denver Gas & Electric company; Gov. H. A. Buchtel, Mayor Speer and many other Denver men were aboard. A party of Boulder people, including the mayor of that place, came to Denver to make the trip on the electric line.

LIST OF STATIONS.

The stations on the new line are Globeville, Dewey, Westminster, Anstees, Semper, Churches, Broomfield, Burns Junction, Denver & Interurban Junction, Superior, Marshall (branch from here to

F. Vincent, assistant chief engineer of the C. & S. and D. & I.; T. S. McMurray, vice president of the Denver & Interurban railroad; C. L. Wellington, traffic manager of the C. & S.; J. D. Welch, general superintendent of the C. & S.; W. A. Webb, assistant to the vice president of the C. & S.; E. E. Hartman, superintendent of the D. & I.; J. L. Israel, tax agent of the C. & S.; R. H. Doolittle, claim agent of the C. & S.; H. S. Crocker, consulting engineer of the C. & S.; T. E. Fisher, general passenger agent of the

pany; A. T. Herr, Frederick Ross, president of the Denver real estate exchange; W. P. McPhee, president of the Colorado Manufacturers' association; F. D. Fowler, president of the Eldorado Springs Resort company; Wolfe Londoner; W. A. Garner, secretary of the Eldorado Springs Resort company; Judge Harry P. Gamble of Boulder; W. H. Allison, president of the First National bank of Boulder; Henry Broadhurst; J. B. Hunter, engineer to the Denver board of public works; C. L. Ossem, and representatives of the Denver and Boulder press.

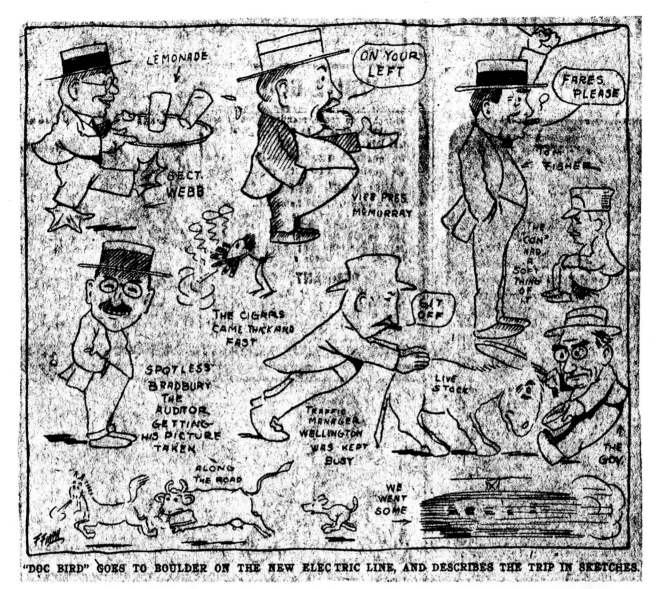

"DOC BIRD" GOES TO BOULDER ON THE NEW ELECTRIC LINE, AND DESCRIBES THE TRIP IN SKETCHES.

The opening of the D & I was a major news event so the *Denver Post* sent a cartoonist on the inaugural run to present his view of the trip along with the news story. A large crowd greeted the arrival of the first train at Boulder, seen parked at the station.—*CRRM*

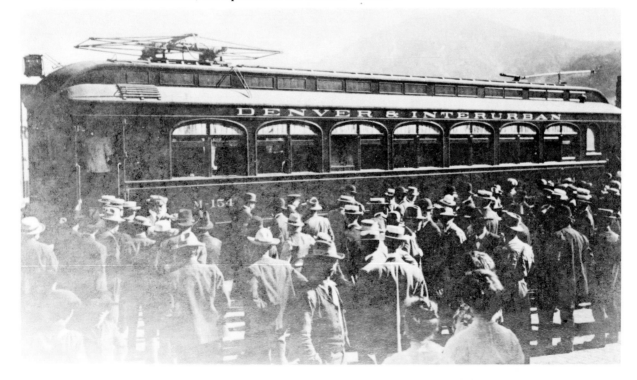

The inaugural special has stopped at Semper and the guests are taking the opportunity to enjoy this fine summer afternoon, June 23, 1908.—CRRM

The electrification on the line along Pearl Street in Boulder had not yet been activated by opening day because certain equipment for the substation which supplied the 550-volt DC power for the city running had not yet been installed. The C & S used a steam engine for the next several days to tow the interurbans into the Boulder depot as in these photos after the arrival of the first D & I car.— *Both, R.H. Kindig Collection.*

Rates from Globeville and Boulder

BETWEEN GLOBEVILLE AND	One Way	ROUND TRIP		FAMILY TICKETS		Individual
		Date of Sale	Sunday Only	25-Ride 90 Days	50-Ride 90 Days	10-Ride 30 Days
Westminster	.15	.25	......	$2.00	$3.35	$ .95
Anstees	.15	.25	......	2.50	4.10	1.15
Madison	.15	.25	......	2.55	4.25	1.20
Semper	.20	.35	......	3.15	5.25	1.50
Churches	.30	.55	.40	4.15	6.90	1.95
Broomfield	.35	.65	.45	4.85	8.10	2.25
Burns Jct	.35	.65	.50	5.10	8.50	2.40
Louisville Jct	.40	.70	.55	5.70	9.50	2.70
Webb	.40	.70	.60	6.10	10.15	2.85
Louisville	.45	.80	.65	6.95	11.55	3.25
Burkes Spur	.50	.90	.70	7.75	12.90	3.60
Weiserhorn Lake	.60	1.10	.85	8.85	14.75	4.15
Boulder Jct	*.65	*1.20	......	......	......	......
Superior	.50	.90	.70	7.10	11.80	3.30
Mitchell Mine	.55	1.00	.75	8.10	13.50	3.80
Marshall	.60	1.10	.85	8.60	14.30	4.00
Eldorado Springs {	.65	ax1 45 / 1.20	x1.25 / 1.00	9.70	16.20	4.55
Park Avenue	†.65	†1.20	†.95	......	......	......
State University	†.70	†1.25	†1.00	†10.35	†17.35	†4.85
Boulder {	*.70 / †.70	a*1.25 / a†1.25	*1.00 / †1.00	‡10.65	‡17.80	‡5.00
BETWEEN BOULDER AND						
Eldorado Springs {	.20	xa.60 / .35	x.55	3.25	5.40	1.50
Marshall	.15	.25	......	2.10	3.50	1.00
Superior	.25	.45	......	3.60	6.00	1.70
Louisville	.25	.45	......	3.70	6.15	1.75

*Via Louisville.
†Via Marshall.
‡Via Marshall or Louisville.
xWith admission coupon.
aAlso on sale Saturday or Sunday, limited to Sunday or Monday.

Unless otherwise shown, tickets are to be honored via direct line only.

COMMUTATION TICKETS will not be transferable, nor will limits on same be extended on any account.

INDIVIDUAL Commutation Tickets will be honored only for one person (the original purchaser), in whose favor issued, and whose signature should be affixed to contract.

FAMILY Commutation Tickets will be good only for the purchaser whose name appears on the face of the ticket, his wife, his children bearing the family name, and one domestic servant. Positively for no others.

Within a month after the first run the Eldorado Springs branch had been electrified and management had settled on running times and scheduling, permitting release of the first permanent timetable dated July 27, 1908. While scheduling adjustments were made and the number of round trips was later reduced, in general the scheduling pattern changed little over the years.— *DPL*

DENVER TO ELDORADO SPRINGS, LOUISVILLE AND BOULDER—All Trains Daily.

Miles	STATIONS	Via Marshall	Via Louisville	Via Marshall	Via Louisville	Via Marshall	Via Louisville	Via Marshall	Via Louisville	Via Marshall	Via Louisville	Via Marshall	Via Louisville	Via Marshall	Via Louisville	Via Marshall	Via Louisville
0	Denver (Sixteenth and Arapahoe Streets) Lv	7.00 AM	8.00 AM	9.00 AM	10.00 AM	11.00 AM	12.00	1.00 PM	2.00 PM	3.00 PM	4.00 PM	5.00 PM	6.00 PM	7.00 PM	8.00 PM	10.00 PM	11.30 PM
3	Globeville Lv	7.15	8.15	9.15	10.15	11.15	12.15	1.15	2.15	3.15	4.15	5.15	6.15	7.15	8.15	10.15	11.45
5	Dewey	7.20	8.20	9.19	10.20	11.20	12.20	1.20	2.20	3.20	4.20	5.20	6.20	7.20	8.20	10.20	11.50
7	Westminster	7.25	8.25	9.22	10.25	11.25	12.25	1.25	2.25	3.25	4.25	5.25	6.25	7.25	8.25	10.25	11.55
8	Anstees	7.27	8.27	9.25	10.27	11.27	12.27	1.27	2.27	3.27	4.27	5.27	6.27	7.27	8.27	10.27	11.57
11	Semper	7.29	8.29	9.28	10.29	11.29	12.29	1.29	2.29	3.29	4.29	5.29	6.29	7.29	8.29	10.29	11.59 PM
13	Churches	7.34	8.34	9.34	10.34	11.34	12.34	1.34	2.34	3.34	4.34	5.34	6.34	7.34	8.34	10.34	12.04 AM
14	Broomfield	7.38	8.38	9.38	10.38	11.38	12.38	1.38	2.38	3.38	4.38	5.38	6.38	7.38	8.38	10.38	12.08
15	Burns Junction	7.40	8.40	9.40	10.40	11.40	12.40	1.40	2.40	3.40	4.40	5.40	6.40	7.40	8.40	10.40	12.10
15	D. & I. Junction Ar	7.42 AM	8.42	9.42	10.42	11.42	12.42	1.42 PM	2.42	3.42	4.42 PM	5.42	6.42 PM	7.42	8.42 PM	10.42	12.12 AM
16	Louisville Junction Ar	7.43 AM		9.43		11.43		1.43 PM		3.43 PM		5.43 PM		7.43 PM		10.43 PM	
19	Superior	7.49		9.49		11.49		1.49		3.49		5.49		7.49		10.54	
22	Mitchell Mine	7.54		10.02		11.54		1.54		3.54		5.54		7.54		10.54 PM	
23	Marshall Ar	7.56 AM		10.04 AM		11.56 AM		1.56 PM		3.56 PM		5.56 PM		7.56 PM		10.56 PM	
26	Eldorado Springs Ar	8.07 AM		10.15 AM		12.13 PM		2.13 PM		4.13 PM		6.13 PM		8.13 PM		11.07 PM	
26	Eldorado Springs Lv	7.45 AM		9.52 AM		11.30 AM		1.30 PM		3.30 PM		5.30 PM		7.30 PM		10.45 PM	
28	University Ar	8.03 AM		10.11 AM		12.03 PM		2.03 PM		4.03 PM		6.03 PM		8.03 PM		11.03 PM	
29	Boulder Ar	8.08 AM		10.16 AM		12.08 PM		2.08 PM		4.08 PM		6.08 PM		8.08 PM		11.08 PM	
15	D. & I. Junction Lv				10.42 AM		12.42 PM		2.42 PM		4.42 PM		6.42 PM		8.42 PM		12.12 AM
16	Webb Ar				10.44		12.44		2.44		4.44		6.44		8.44		12.14
18	Louisville				10.53		12.53		2.53		4.52		6.53		8.53		12.19
20	Burkes				10.57		12.57		2.57		4.58		6.57		8.57		12.25
23	Weiserhorn				11.05		1.05		3.05		5.03		7.03		9.03		12.31
24	Culbertson				11.07		1.07		3.07		5.05		7.05		9.05		12.33
26	Inland				11.11		1.11		3.11		5.07		7.07		9.07		12.35
27	Boulder Junction				11.15		1.15		3.15		5.10		7.10		9.10		12.38
29	Boulder Ar				11.20 AM		1.20 PM		3.20 PM		5.15 PM		7.15 PM		9.15 PM		12.43 AM

BOULDER TO ELDORADO SPRINGS, LOUISVILLE AND DENVER—All Trains Daily.

Miles	STATIONS	Via Marshall	Via Louisville	Via Marshall	Via Louisville	Via Marshall	Via Louisville	Via Marshall	Via Louisville	Via Marshall	Via Louisville	Via Marshall	Via Louisville	Via Marshall	Via Louisville	Via Marshall	Via Louisville
0	Boulder Lv	6.30 AM		9.30 AM		11.30 AM		1.30 PM		3.30 PM		5.30 PM		7.30 PM		9.30 PM	
1	University	6.33		9.33		11.33		1.33		3.33		5.33		7.33		9.33	
6	Marshall Ar	6.40 AM		9.40 AM		11.40 AM		1.40 PM		3.40 PM		5.40 PM		7.40 PM		9.40 PM	
9	Eldorado Springs Ar	6.51 AM		9.51 AM		11.51 AM		1.51 PM		3.51 PM		5.51 PM		7.51 PM		9.51 PM	
9	Eldorado Springs Lv	6.30 AM		9.30 AM		11.30 AM		1.30 PM		3.30 PM		5.30 PM		7.30 PM		9.30 PM	
7	Mitchell Mine Lv	6.42		9.42		11.42		1.42		3.42		5.42		7.42		9.42	
10	Superior	6.49		9.49		11.49		1.49		3.49		5.49		7.49		9.49	
13	Louisville Junction Lv	6.55		9.55		11.55		1.55		3.55		5.55		7.55		9.55	
0	Boulder Lv		6.56 AM		9.02 AM		11.02 AM		1.02 PM		3.02 PM		5.02 PM		7.02 PM		9.02 PM
2	Boulder Junction		6.58		9.04		11.04		1.04		3.04		5.04		7.04		9.04
3	Inland		7.00		9.05		11.05		1.05		3.05		5.05		7.05		9.05
5	Culbertson		7.04		9.08		11.08		1.08		3.08		5.08		7.08		9.08
6	Weiserhorn		7.10		9.13		12.00 PM		2.04		4.04		6.04		8.04		9.13
9	Burkes		7.13		9.18		12.04		2.10		4.10		6.10		8.10		9.18
11	Louisville		7.15		9.20		12.13		2.13		4.13		6.13		8.13		9.14
13	Webb		7.20		9.22		12.15		2.15		4.15		6.15		8.15		9.20
14	D. & I. Junction Ar		7.25 AM		9.30 AM		12.20 PM		2.20 PM		4.20 PM		6.20 PM		8.20 PM		9.25 PM
14	D. & I. Junction Lv	6.56 AM	7.02 AM	9.56 AM	11.02 AM	11.56 AM	1.02 PM	1.56 PM	3.04 PM	3.56 PM	5.04 PM	5.56 PM	7.04 PM	7.56 PM	9.04 PM	9.56 PM	12.03 AM
15	Burns Junction	6.58	7.04	9.58	11.04	11.58	1.04	1.58	3.05	3.58	5.05	5.58	7.05	7.58	9.05	9.58	12.05
16	Broomfield	7.00	7.08	10.00	11.05	12.00 PM	1.08	2.00	3.08	4.00	5.08	6.00	7.08	8.00	9.08	10.00	12.08
18	Churches	7.04	7.13	10.04	11.13	12.04	1.13	2.04	3.13	4.04	5.13	6.04	7.13	8.04	9.13	10.04	12.10
21	Semper	7.10	7.18	10.09	11.14	12.10	1.14	2.10	3.16	4.10	5.16	6.10	7.16	8.10	9.14	10.10	12.13
22	Anstees	7.13	7.20	10.12	11.16	12.13	1.16	2.13	3.18	4.13	5.18	6.13	7.18	8.13	9.18	10.13	12.16
24	Westminster	7.15	7.22	10.14	11.20	12.15	1.20	2.15	3.20	4.15	5.20	6.15	7.20	8.15	9.20	10.15	12.18
26	Dewey	7.20	7.26	10.20	11.25	12.20	1.25	2.20	3.25	4.20	5.25	6.20	7.25	8.20	9.25	10.20	12.20
29	Globeville Ar	7.25	7.30	10.25	11.25	12.25	1.25	2.25	3.25	4.25	5.25	6.25	7.25	8.25	9.25	10.25	12.25
29	Denver (Sixteenth and Arapahoe Streets) Ar	7.40 AM	9.45 AM	10.40 AM	11.40 AM	12.40 PM	1.40 PM	2.40 PM	3.40 PM	4.40 PM	5.40 PM	6.40 PM	7.40 PM	8.40 PM	9.40 PM	10.40 PM	12.40 AM

NOTICE.—All tickets read to and from Globeville. Transfer or 5 cents will be collected between Sixteenth and Arapahoe Streets and Globeville. In going from Denver ask Tramway Conductor for transfer to Globeville, and on arriving Denver for transfer to any part of the city.

20

The opening of the Denver & Interurban brought a new prosperity along its route. Real estate promoters advertised fast electric service to Broomfield—which they attempted but failed to rename Lakeview Valley—and Boulder merchants were thrilled to have the interurbans drop passengers on Pearl Street. For Eldorado Springs the purchase and electrification of their branch line by the D & I meant a boom each summer. In this scene the view is west on Pearl Street at Fourteenth with the Masonic Temple on the left and the courthouse on the right. The track turning the corner belongs to the city streetcar line.—*All CRRM*

Dept. No. ....   Treas. No. ....   Audit No. **353**

The Denver & Interurban Railroad Company.

Charge ....   To .... The Continental Trust Company, ... Dr.

....   353   Of .... Denver, Colorado. ....

....   Pay .... Same

Month of ....*Aug*............... 190 7   Address .... Same

For interest on deferred payments for purchase of bonds of The Eldorado Springs Railway Co., to Sept. 26th, 1907.			35	00	
For interest on deferred payments for purchase of capital stock of The Eldorado Springs Railway Co., to Sept. 26th, 1907.			84	41	119	41

DENVER & INTERURBAN CONDUCTOR

Letters Gilt.

Gilt

Black Silk

Gilt

Band 25" long

Hat Band
Denver & Interurban Pass. Conductors

Sept 21-09.

Sketch
M. 31.

A series of sketches were made and designs selected for hats and badges for D & I crewmen. When new badges were ordered from the Denver Novelty Works & Electric Co., they cost all of fifty cents each.—*CRRM*

J. W. MACRUM, PRESIDENT   GOODS SENT BY MAIL AT PURCHASERS RISK   E. W. MANNING, SEC'Y AND TREAS

FOLIO_____   DENVER, COLO., **Jany. 4th. 1915.**

M. the Denver & Interurban R. R. Co.
    Storekeeper, 23rd. & Market Sts. City.

To **The Denver Novelty Works & Electric Co.** DR

SEALS, STENCILS, STEEL STAMPS, BRASS AND ALUMINUM
TRADE CHECKS, BADGES, CHECK PROTECTORS, NUMBERING
MACHINES, KEYS AND KEY BLANKS, &Co.

BRASS SIGNS.   BRASS TABLETS.   ETCHED GLASS SIGNS.
RUBBER STAMPS, RUBBER TYPE AND SIGN MARKERS

ELECTRICAL SUPPLIES

PRIVATE LINE AND INTERCOMMUNICATING TELEPHONES

TELEPHONE MAIN 809   SIGNATURE   511 STOUT ST.

8	Conductor Badges,	Order 24-18	@ 50¢	net.	$4.00

APPROVED

Elec. Engr. & Trainmaster.

. B.

Prices Correct

ORIGINAL

D & I R R
4152

THE COLORADO & SOUTHERN RAILWAY CO.
TELEGRAM

OPERATORS ARE REQUIRED TO WRITE ALL TELEGRAMS IN INK.   The TIME filed as well as DATE filed must be transmitted.
Office Signal, To or From, Sender, Receiver, and the Time Sent or Received MUST BE SHOWN on all Telegrams.   Telegrams for parties on trains
(except those addressed to train men) must be placed in envelopes.

Time Filed   7/6/08

Mr. J. D. Welsh,
     Denver, Colo.

         Please send me four Denver & Interurban badges for use for the electricians Headricks and Edmunds and their assistants. Want them to go over the line and see that all cars are working properly after set up before leaving us. Badges will be turned in as soon as they are through with them.

12:35   H. C. VanBuskirk.

William H. Edmunds was one of four men sent by Westinghouse to supervise installation of the electrical equipment on the D & I. After the line opened the D & I wanted to be sure everything was in perfect working order before the experts left so requested the men from Westinghouse ride the line for several days and an order was prepared to supply them the necessary identification badges.—CRRM

These crewmen are smartly attired and look proud to be in charge of this inspection run about the time of the line's opening. Most of the men came from service on the C & S and thus were experienced on the route.—Edmunds Collection

23

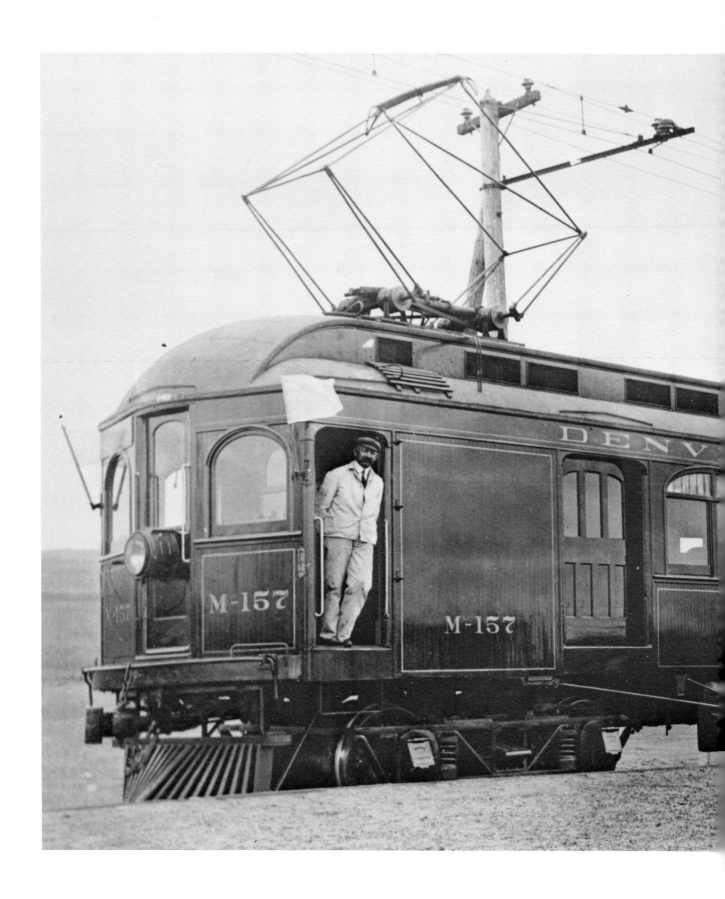

The M-157 was brand new when operated on this inspection trip probably just prior to opening day. The photo was taken by Andrew Whiteford who held various positions on the D & I including trainmaster and was a close friend of General Manager William D. Edmunds for whom he took numerous photos which appear in this book from the Edmunds collection. The motorman is Fred Spencer while standing at the rear from left to right are Conductor Grenamyre, Line Foreman Hardcastle, Shop Foreman Williams and Electrical Engineer Darlington. The location is D & I Junction.—*Edmunds Collection.*

Electric Transportation to Eldorado Springs, Boulder and the Glacier Region.

13 - Electric Trains Daily Each Way - 13

Quick, Clean, Comfortable and Inexpensive. High speed, modern Electric trains from Denver Union Station nearly every hour for that delightful region about Eldorado Springs, Boulder and the Glacier region. A more comfortable trip cannot be imagined.

Very low round trip fares.

From Boulder you can visit the famed Glacier region and at Eldorado Springs you can enjoy swimming in the Radium pool or live in a delightful Mountain Cottage.

Interurban Trains leave Union Station.

For descriptive matter write

C. W. RICHARDS, General Passenger Agent
Denver & Interurban R. R.
1654 Broadway
Main 805—Branch 125

Interurbans to Boulder
The Route and the Schedule

The Route

The Denver & Interurban Railroad lay east of the Rockies. It was built in that part of Colorado where the Great Plains meet the towering wall of mountains known as the Front Range. This land, from Denver northward toward Wyoming, is a semi-arid landscape of gently rolling hills and flat lands.

Denver sits at an elevation of 5,280 feet, while Boulder is only slightly higher at 5,430. The maximum grade on the thirty-three route miles of electified trackage connecting them was 1.25 percent. The D & I faced no geographical obstacles in its route, and only entered the Rocky Mountain foothills on the branch to Eldorado Springs. Most of this route predated the D & I electrification. It was established by the Union Pacific, Denver & Gulf Railroad, taken over by the Colorado & Southern, and then operated by the D & I under lease and trackage rights agreements.

The D & I became known as the "Kite Route" because when viewed on a map, its route resembled a kite on a string. Catchy nicknames had advertising value and management did not ignore that. The nickname was officially adopted and appeared on timetables, letterheads, and even the sides of rolling stock.

Denver was a major business center with a population of 213,000 in 1910 which grew by 20 percent to 256,000 by 1920. It was also home to the offices of the D & I, which were located in the Railway Exchange building. The original downtown Denver terminal was located on Arapahoe Street at Sixteenth, but on May 12, 1910, the D & I began using the Denver Tramway's Interurban Loop. Use of this terminal was shared with forty-two-inch narrow gauge interurban cars of the Tramway and standard gauge cars of the Denver & Intermountain Railroad. The Tramway line ran to Golden via one route and the D & IM served it via another route. The D & IM was a division of the

The sign on the front of M-157 reads "This car for Boulder via Louisville." On the left car 22 of the Denver & Intermountain standard gauge line loads prior to departure for Golden in this scene at the Interurban Loop in 1912.—*CRRM*

The start of the D & I's private right-of-way is seen here as the track leaves Washington Street near Fifty-third Avenue, a block beyond the end of the Denver Tramway line. Retreat Park, site of the Globeville wreck is just out of view to the right.—CRRM

Tramway. Interurban Loop consisted of double tracks on Arapahoe, Thirteenth Street, Curtis, and Fifteenth Street, with four station tracks on private property between Fourteenth and Fifteenth. The ticket office was in an adjacent building. This terminal was especially convenient to riders because it was right across the street from the Tramway's Central Loop. That terminal served as the transfer point for many of the Tramway's forty-two-inch gauge city lines.

From the loop, the D & I utilized the double tracked Tramway Globeville Route, north on Arapahoe to Twenty-third. It turned west on Twenty-third, running past the D & I shops and across the Twenty-third Street viaduct to Fox Street. It ran on Fox Street to Forty-fourth on a private right-of-way to Forty-fifth, and east on Forty-fifth to Washington. On Washington, it ran north past the Denver Union Stockyards to Globeville, a neighborhood named for the old Globe Smelter. The Denver & Interurban's rented station at 5126 Washington marked the end of the Tramway line and the beginning of Kite route property. North of the depot, near Retreat Park, cars switched from 550 volts DC to 11,000 volts AC and entered a private right-of-way. Beyond Globeville, all operation was under the authority of the Colorado & Southern dispatcher.

From Globeville, the line swung around the Retreat Park hill to enter the Colorado & Southern right-of-way at Modern Junction. From Modern Junction to Webb Junction the D & I ran on the northeast track of a double track line. Steam trains used the other track. This separation was necessary in order to limit the amount of schedule in-

terference caused by C & S freight and passenger trains, narrow gauge Denver, Boulder & Western ore and passenger trains and assorted Burlington Railroad trains. The Burlington used the C & S route from Denver to Burns Junction, while the DB & W used it all the way from Denver to Boulder, permitting through ore shipments to the Argo smelter. In a move to avoid interference with steam operations the C & S required that all catenary support poles, guy wires, sidings and stations be located on the north and east side of the D & I track. The term "catenary" refers to the overhead electrification system.

The Modern to Webb portion of the line served the towns of Westminster, which had a population of 235 in 1920 and Broomfield, which had a population of 167. Westminster was the junction point for a 1.8 mile branch to Westminster University. This line was completed late in 1910. It was operated each year from September through May, when school was in session. A rail bus was substituted for interurban service during the 1913-14 school year and the line was abandoned due to low traffic in 1914.

From Webb to Boulder, via Louisville, the electric cars shared use of the tracks with the C & S and the DB & W. Louisville was a coal mining town, and in 1920 it had a population of 1,799. The town of Lafayette lay a few miles east of Louisville. It was served by a C & S steam local which brought passengers to the D & I. Lafayette was also a coal mining town and had a population of 1,815. It was the site of the coal fired power plant which provided electricity for the D & I.

One-half mile east of Boulder lay the wye shaped

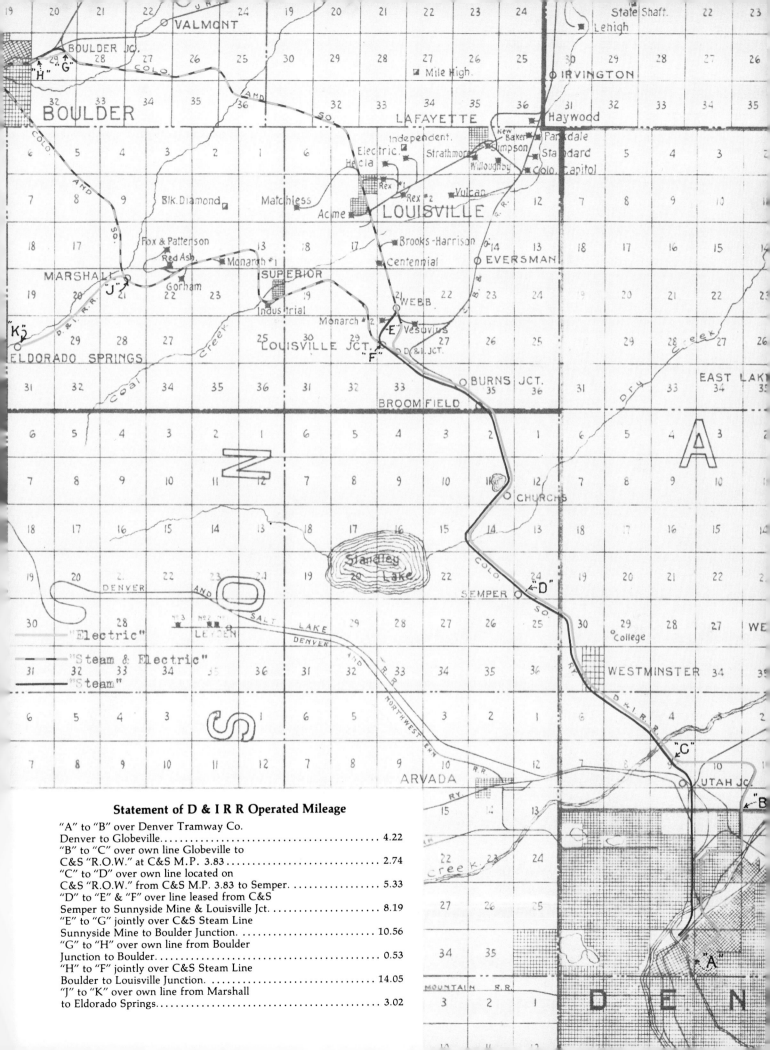

Statement of D & I R R Operated Mileage

"A" to "B" over Denver Tramway Co.
Denver to Globeville.. 4.22
"B" to "C" over own line Globeville to
C&S "R.O.W." at C&S M.P. 3.83............................ 2.74
"C" to "D" over own line located on
C&S "R.O.W." from C&S M.P. 3.83 to Semper............ 5.33
"D" to "E" & "F" over line leased from C&S
Semper to Sunnyside Mine & Louisville Jct............... 8.19
"E" to "G" jointly over C&S Steam Line
Sunnyside Mine to Boulder Junction....................... 10.56
"G" to "H" over own line from Boulder
Junction to Boulder... 0.53
"H" to "F" jointly over C&S Steam Line
Boulder to Louisville Junction............................... 14.05
"J" to "K" over own line from Marshall
to Eldorado Springs... 3.02

Boulder Junction. One leg of the wye carried traffic north toward Fort Collins, while the other carried traffic to Boulder. Following a realignment of trackage used by the C & S and the D & I, this location was renamed ARA.

In Boulder, a town of 11,000, the D & I ran down Pearl Street to a depot at Twelfth, then followed Twelfth to the C & S line near the mouth of Boulder Canyon. The narrow gauge Denver, Boulder & Western route left C & S right-of-way at this point. The DB & W went up Boulder Canyon to the towns of Ward, Sunset and Eldora. Narrow gauge trains ceased operating to Denver in 1916, when the C & S cancelled the DB & W's Boulder to Denver trackage rights.

From Boulder, the Kite route passed through the University of Colorado campus and proceeded to the town of Marshall. Marshall had a population of 707 in 1920 and was the junction point for the three-mile long branch, running to the Eldorado Springs Resort.

The resort was built entirely on private land inside of South Boulder Canyon. It was primarily a summer vacation spot with little permanent population. Local developers started the resort in 1904. It featured a giant outdoor swimming pool which was heated to a constant temperature of seventy-six degrees by an adjacent hot spring. With the impending start of interurban service to the area, the resort's owners sensed that money could be made if their resort were more accessible to the public. In 1907, they laid rails down to the C & S line at Marshall and christened their new operation the Eldorado Springs Railway. The rolling stock consisted of automobiles running on railroad wheels and the line was nicknamed "The Automobile Road." The developers built a large guest hotel in 1908, and the D & I electrified the Eldorado Springs Railway track in order to bring in

the guests. The D & I purchased the line in fall 1908, and Eldorado Springs became the highest point reached by the D & I. Its elevation is 6,000 feet and the line from Marshall had a steady two percent grade. At a time when accessible resorts were few and heated swimming pools were rare, Eldorado Springs was a hit. It attracted as many as two thousand people on weekends through the summer. Among its guests in 1916 was a honeymooning twenty-six-year-old Second Lieutenant named Dwight D. Eisenhower and his new wife, Mamie. It is not known whether they arrived on the D & I or a C & S steam train.

Along the line from Marshall to Louisville Junction was the town of Superior. Its population in 1920 was 532. The line from Marshall completed the loop through Boulder by making connections with the rest of the line at Louisville Junction and D & I Junction.

When the D & I was initially electrified, there was a desire to separate interurban traffic from steam traffic as much as possible. To facilitate this, the D & I line from Denver split at D & I Junction, while the steam line split at Louisville Junction. Interurban cars travelling via Marshall passed through D & I Junction and Louisville Junction. Those travelling via Louisville used D & I Junction and Webb Junction. After a few years, it became apparent that three junctions and three sets of train order operators were performing work that could easily be handled by one. The steam track was then electrified from Louisville Junction to Webb. The unnecessary D & I Junction and Webb Junction were then eliminated. Louisville Junction was later renamed Coalton.

Other route changes included a 1917 move from the streets of Boulder to the C & S line and, in 1922, a move from the Tramway route to a line into Union Station.

When the D & I began running from Union Station it used the Burlington's line just east of the C & S main line, seen here at Forty-eighth Avenue crossing with stacks of the Denver Sewer and Clay Pipe Company in the background. The young ladies appear to be waiting for the interurban.—CRRM

Dewey

The M-152 waits for a meet in this, the only known photo at Dewey, just east of Utah Junction.—*CRRM*

A pair of transfers provide a full listing of stations along the D & I.
—*CRRM*

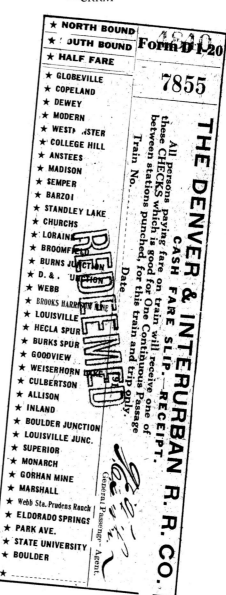

★ NORTH BOUND	FORM D I-20
	SERIES 2
1 DENVER	
2 FOX STREET	38874
2a BURLINGTON SHOPS	
3 UTAH JUNCTION	
4 MODERN	
4a FEDERAL BOULEVARD	
5 WESTMINSTER	
6 COLLEGE HILL	
7 SEMPER	
8 BARZOI	
9 STANDLEY LAKE	
10 MANDALAY	
11 LORAINE	
12 BROOMFIELD	
13 BURNS JUNCTION	
14 COALTON	
14a SPICERS	
15 SUPERIOR	
16 CROWN	
17 GORHAM	
18 MARSHALL	
19 BASE LINE	
20 UNIVERSITY	
21 BOULDER	
★ HALF FARE	
22 LIGNITE	
23 CENTENNIAL	
24 LOUISVILLE	
25 HECLA	
26 WHITE	
27 GOODVIEW	
28 WEISERHORN	
29 LAKESIDE	
30 ARA	
31 PRUDENS	
32 ELDORADO SP'GS	
★ SOUTH BOUND	

Train No. ....

Cash Fare Slip — RECEIPT. CHECKS which is good for One Continuous Passage between stations punched, for this train and trip only.

Date .... 19........

THE DENVER & INTERURBAN R. R. CO.

CURRAN, St L.

All persons paying fare on train will receive one of these

★ NORTH BOUND	
★ SOUTH BOUND	FORM D I-20
★ HALF FARE	
★ GLOBEVILLE	7855
★ COPELAND	
★ DEWEY	
★ MODERN	
★ WESTMINSTER	
★ COLLEGE HILL	
★ ANSTEES	
★ MADISON	
★ SEMPER	
★ BARZOI	
★ STANDLEY LAKE	
★ CHURCHS	
★ LORAINE	
★ BROOMFIELD	
★ BURNS JUNCTION	
★ D. & JUNCTION	
★ WEBB	
★ BROOKS HARRISON LINE	
★ LOUISVILLE	
★ HECLA SPUR	
★ BURKS SPUR	
★ GOODVIEW	
★ WEISERHORN LAKE	
★ CULBERTSON	
★ ALLISON	
★ INLAND	
★ BOULDER JUNCTION	
★ LOUISVILLE JUNC.	
★ SUPERIOR	
★ MONARCH	
★ GORHAN MINE	
★ MARSHALL	
★ Webb Sta. Prudens Ranch	
★ ELDORADO SPRINGS	
★ PARK AVE.	
★ STATE UNIVERSITY	
★ BOULDER	
★	

REDEEMED

Train No. ....

CASH FARE SLIP — RECEIPT. between stations punched, for this train and trip only. these CHECKS which is good for One Continuous Passage

Date ....

All persons paying fare on train will receive one of

THE DENVER & INTERURBAN R. R. CO.

General Passenger Agent.

Westminster College Branch

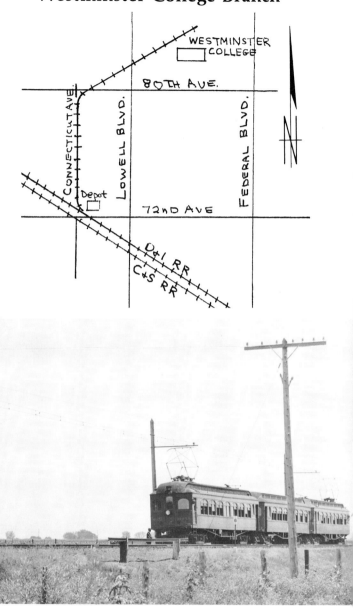

In this set of photos a three car train is seen near Federal Boulevard just east of Westminster. The photos were taken by the D & I to simulate conditions during a serious grade crossing accident a few days earlier. Drivers failed to realize the speed of the interurbans and without the usual steam engine smoke see med more apt to miss their approach.
—CRRM

The picturesque Westminster station was located just north of present day west Seventy-second Avenue at Connecticut Avenue (today Bradburn Blvd.). The Westminster College branch began at this point, curving northward in front of the buildings on the left and up Connecticut Avenue. L.C. McClure took this photo shortly after the line opened, while at left M-151 has paused at the station in this 1909 photo by Andrew Whitford.—*Above, DPL; Left, Edmunds Collection*

Westminster College Branch

One of the least known and shortest lived branch lines in Colorado was the Westminster College branch of the D & I. In 1908 the Presbyterian church established Westminster College on a high point of land north of Denver known as Crown Point. The imposing college building still stands although after financial problems forced the original college to close in 1917, the facility was sold to the Pillar of Fire Church which continues to operate both an elementary and secondary school and a college under the name Belleview College and Preparatory School.

Soon after opening the college officials requested the D & I build a branch to serve them directly and avoid the mile walk from the Westminster station to the college at Eighty-second Avenue and Julian Street. The D & I agreed and in August 1910 was granted a franchise by the Adams County Board of Commissioners for right-of-way on a county road known then as Connecticut Avenue but which is now Bradburn Boulevard. On September 9, 1910 an A.F.E. (authority for expenditure) was issued for construction of 9500 feet of track including grades slightly in excess of 5 percent and costing an estimated $22,400.

A shortage of standard gauge ties brought a decision to obtain surplus narrow gauge pine ties from the South Park division, these being considered satisfactory for the light traffic the line would bear. The track was completed October 14, but electrification was delayed until early November awaiting delivery of certain supplies. When the job was completed it was under estimate at $21,014.52.

(Continued on page 35.)

The Westminster College branch ran north on Connecticut Avenue (now Bradburn Boulevard) as shown at upper left about 1912. The line can be seen approaching the college from the west in this unusual photo taken from the building's tower. The college building appears today little changed from the view above taken about 1910. During 1913-14 the college used this rail bus, posed at the Westminster station, in an attempt to maintain service when the line had deteriorated to the point that the D & I could no longer safely operate heavy interurbans. On a fine day in 1911 or 1912 students and faculty posed at the college but the interurban is not the M-158 which usually provided service, indicating it may have been a special run through from Denver.—*Above, DPL; Others, Matilda Campbell Collection*

As work was being completed C & S Vice-President Parker and General Superintendent Welsh studied the questions of who would operate the line, charges to be made and what equipment to use. The following major points were contained in the agreement signed with the college on November 21, 1910.

1. The college to pay 5% interest on the construction cost of $21,014.52.

2. The D & I to furnish a car at no cost until June 1, 1911 after which negotiations would determine a fair rental or the college could obtain its own car.

3. The D & I to provide power at a cost of 24¢ per round trip.

4. All maintenance on track, overhead and car the responsibility of the D & I.

5. The college to employ a motorman who would be examined by the superintendent and general foreman of the electrical department.

6. The college to keep all fares collected on the branch.

College President Salem G. Pattison sent Ward Allen to be examined as motorman but due to his very poor eyesight and complete lack of understanding of mechanical equipment the D & I asked for another selection and this time W.B. Pattison, son of the president was selected and approved by the railroad.

At 8:00 A.M. on November 17, 1910, M-158 was run from the barn in Denver to the college to begin service, and except for a few days on two occasions during servicing and repairs, the car was used throughout the life of the branch. To provide a standby motorman the college pump station engineer, a Mr. B. Hester, was also trained by the D & I.

Only two serious problems arose in the short life of the Westminster College branch. The first occurred on January 16, 1911 when M-158 ran out of control at speeds of up to sixty miles per hour down the 5 percent grade, through the derail and twenty-two rail lengths beyond on the ground. An investigation determined that one of President Pattison's sons, but not the one trained as motorman, had ordered Hester to collect fares while he took a turn at the controls. There was also talk that he had some women with him in the cab. He promptly picked up too much speed and Hester attempted to stop, but too late. There were severe flat spots on all wheels, damage to the sanders and brake rigging problems, but the car was back in service in a few days with the college paying for the repairs and with a letter from the president to the effect this would not happen again.

The other incident occurred at 1:24 P.M. on May 11, 1913 when the power was cut from Globeville to Boulder Junction and the powerhouse was unable to restore it because the circuit breakers continually cut out. An alert operator at Westminster located the problem. The branch line car had been parked by the station with the pantograph up and an insulator had shattered causing a short resulting in sparks and smoke coming from the roof. The doors were locked but the fast thinking operator found a rope and managed to catch hold of the pantograph and pull it down. Power was restored at 2:10 P.M. but schedules were mixed up for the rest of the afternoon. D & I officials were most unhappy with this careless handling of their car.

In March 1911 a passenger count indicated an average of sixty-three persons rode the car per day and most did continue their journey on the main line. The D & I wanted this business but attempted to locate a smaller car for the branch. The use of a Fort Collins car was investigated but the cost of converting it to run on the Kite Route's single phase AC power system was $5,250.00. The college then arranged for William Evans of the Denver Tramway to offer one of their city cars but this too would be too costly to convert to the AC power system. A partial solution was reached when the college agreed it was not necessary to operate during the summer thus freeing the D & I car for use during the busy Eldorado Springs season.

The college was facing a difficult financial situation and simply could not obtain its own car nor pay the $10.00 a day rental charge the D & I was now requesting. The D & I agreed to continue with only the charge for power but by spring 1913 there was growing concern for the considerable amount of work needed to bring the branch up to good operating condition. On June 12, 1913 the college closed for the summer and M-158 was run into Denver; it would never return to the line.

Superintendent Welsh reported to Vice-President Parker that the cost to put the line in condition would be $3,599.75 and wrote on August 16, "I am not disposed to put a car on there again this following year, especially as it will cost so much to put the line in servicable condition."

Since the D & I was unwilling to provide a car, the college obtained a gasoline powered rail bus probably late in 1913. Little is known regarding its operation except that Henry D. Gregory, a member of a long-time Westminster family, was the operator. There was no operation after late 1914 and after discussions with the Westminster Board of Trustees gained their approval for abandonment, the line was quickly taken up with the task finished on May 4, 1915.

Semper

A Boulder-bound car flying flags indicating a special waits on the siding at Semper as the regular Denver-bound interurban approaches. A short distance beyond, photographer L.C. McClure, about 1910 took this fine shot of the well maintained D & I—C & S double track right-of-way.—*Above, A.A. Paddock Collection; Below, DPL*

This long, straight stretch west of Semper made for fast running and gave a slight blur to this McClure photo circa 1910. The D & I rented right-of-way from the C & S along this portion of its line as indicated by the bill from the U.S. Railroad Administration which operated the C & S—but not the D & I—and most other railroads during World War I.—*CRRM*

Form D&I-1st Rev.-6-18-7M.

BILL COLLECTIBLE

DEPARTMENT NO. D-5735

DATE September 1 1919

WHEN REMITTING PLEASE QUOTE

AUDIT NO. 9004

RECORDED IN Sept 1919

The Denver & Interurban Railroad Company

ADDRESS Denver - Colorado.

To United States Railroad Administration, Dr.

W. G. McADOO, Director General of Railroads

WALKER D. HINES Colorado & Southern Railroad

REMITTANCE SHOULD BE MADE TO B. F. JAMES, FEDERAL TREASURER, DENVER, COLO.

FOR rent of R of W MP 3.67 to MP 9.0
Semper and joint track and facilities MP 16.96
to Boulder Jct MP 27.56 (via Louisville and
Boulder MP 29.28 to Louisville Jct MP 16.41
(via Marshall) month of September 1919.

Agreement 7-1-08   File 20-D

$617.91

D. & I. R. R.
No. 243
Transmittal.

Distribution
Joint Facility Rent.

FEDERAL ACCOUNT

APPROVED _____ Superintendent

DO NOT ALTER BILL. IF EXCEPTION IS TAKEN, RETURN TO E. I. GRENFELL,
GENERAL AUDITOR, DENVER, COLO., FOR CORRECTION, STATING OBJECTIONS.

AUDITED:

APPROVED FOR COLLECTION:

FOR THE FEDERAL AUDITOR

Assistant Federal Auditor

Broomfield

The M-158 pauses in Broomfield, so named for the boom corn once widely cultivated in the area. L.C. McClure took this view (below) of Broomfield about 1910. By the mid-1980s the same location, now served by the Burlington Northern, is a busy Denver suburb.—*Above, CRRM; Below, DPL*

Louisville Junction   D & I Junction

Louisville Junction—1908—The area known as Louisville Junction actually included three junctions. The original Louisville Junction became D & I Junction and was the point at which the electrified line branched to the north from the C & S; New Louisville Junction was the point at which the C & S main line to Boulder separated from the C & S—D & I joint line via Marshall to Boulder; and the point at which the D & I and the C & S main line to Boulder rejoined was Webb Junction. It soon became obvious that traffic did not require three junctions. The segment from D & I Junction to Webb was abandoned, the C & S line between New Louisville Junction and Webb was electrified and thus only one junction remained, known simply as Louisville Junction.

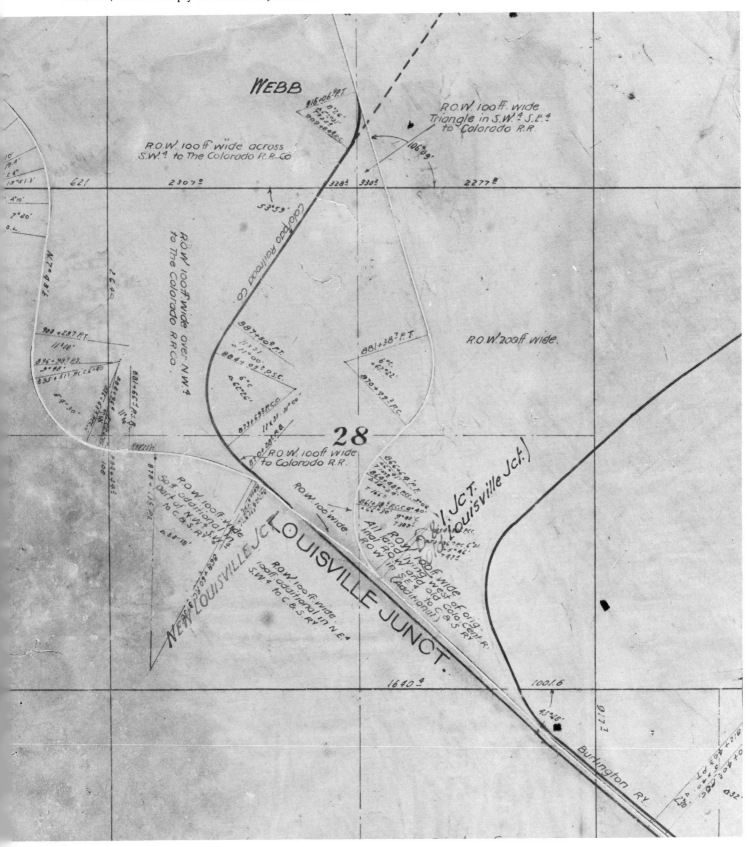

Louisville

This classic scene of the interurban era was taken on an afternoon about 1910 during a three way meet at Louisville. A Boulder-bound car waits next to the station, in the center is a Denver car and on the right C & S engine 303 waits with the Lafayette local.—*R. H. Kindig Collection*

A few years later an almost identical three-way meet as that pictured at left is again captured on film at Louisville, the station has been rebuilt. By the mid-1970s the station at Louisville was but a memory although the railroad remains an important freight line now operating under the Burlington Northern name since that road finally absorbed the C & S in 1982.—*Above, CRRM; Below, Noel Holley*

Superior

The town of Superior was site of busy coal mining operations providing both freight for the C & S and passenger revenue to the D & I. The line is seen a short distance west of Superior at Gorman.— *Aulls photo, E.J. Haley Collection*

The Eldorado Springs branch began in Marshall as seen on this map.—*Public Utilities Commission of Colorado*

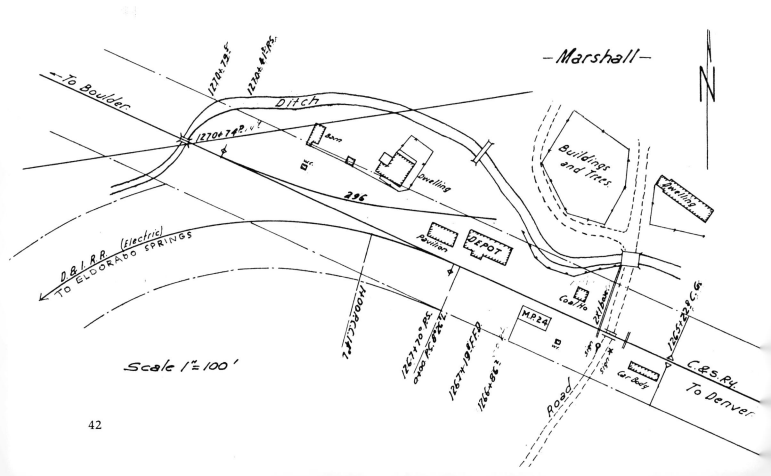

42

Few photos exist of Marshall, but on May 20, 1909, L.C. McClure took this fine view of the town while a steam powered inspection train made a brief stop. The view is northwest toward Boulder and the Eldorado Springs branch begins just off the left of the photo.—*DPL*

From Marshall the D & I ran north to Boulder as seen here about one mile beyond the Eldorado Springs junction at a point known locally as Shanahan's Crossing. The pilot of an interurban can be seen to the right of the track, the result of a recent encounter with an automobile.—*CRRM*

Eldorado Springs Branch

It is a busy day at Eldorado Springs with a steam powered C & S special on the siding, a two car D & I train on the loop along with a lone coach—both most likely specials—and what is probably the regular D & I run alongside the locomotive at the depot.—*E. J. Haley Collection; ticket and folder, CRRM*

ELDORADO SPRINGS

65 Minutes from Work to Play

That's all—65 minutes' ride on The Denver and Interurban electric trains takes you from work and worry of shop, store or office to a delightful place of rest and play.

You can go to Eldorado Springs, have a good day's rest or pleasure and come back the same day.

You can keep your family there, come in to business every day, going back for the evening and night.

You can spend your whole vacation time there, yet be in easy reach of your work or business.

You can enjoy all the pleasures of a mountain retreat, with all the conveniences of city life.

You can live in a private cottage or at the hotel, and in either case at reasonable rates.

The Business Man's Special Train leaves Eldorado Springs daily 6:32 a. m., arriving Denver 7:45 a. m.

ELDORADO SPRINGS

—CRRM

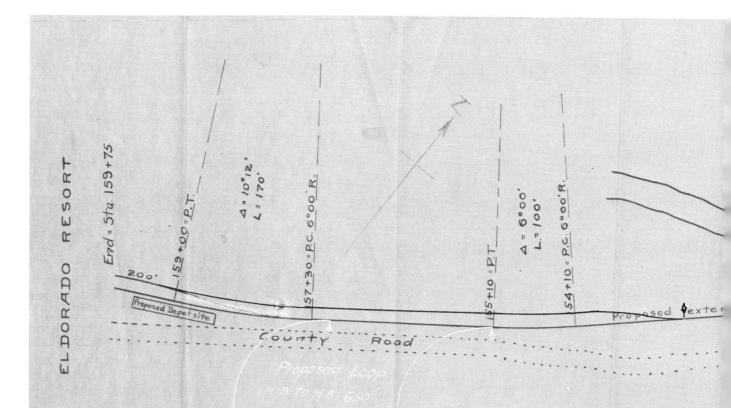

MAP
SHOWING
PROPOSED EXTENSION
OF
ELDORADO SPRINGS R.Y.
SCALE 1" = 100'
OFFICE OF CH.ENG'R. DENVER, APR, 8,'07.

The developers of the Eldorado Springs resort built their own railroad to Marshall in 1907, hoping to eventually sell the line to the D & I. Their strategy worked and the line was electrified by mid-summer, 1908, but prior to electrification these interesting rail cars were used to transport visitors from the resort to Marshall.—*Left, CHS; Right, CLB*

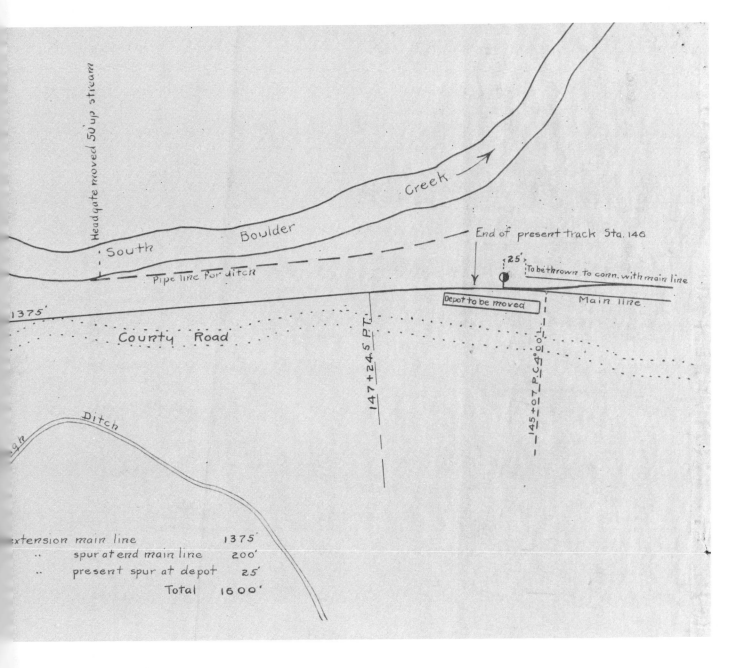

extension main line   1375'
   spur at end main line   200'
   present spur at depot   25'
        Total   1600'

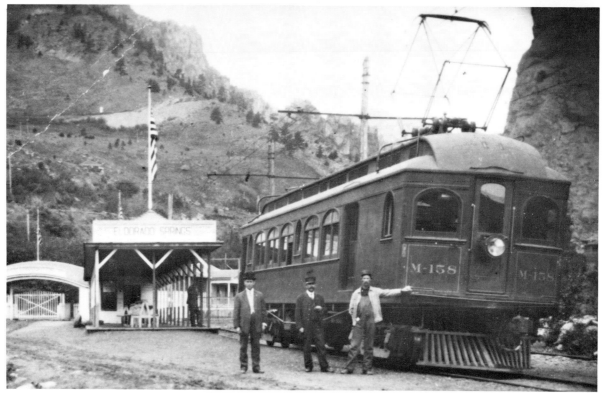

This classic photo of Eldorado Springs was used in countless advertisements to sell the virtues of a visit to the famed resort via the Kite Route.—*Gene C. McKeever Collection*

←A trio of scenes on the Eldorado Springs branch; from top to bottom, a single car approaches on the long passing track, the M-158 prepares to depart during a quiet moment at the resort, and a three-car train awaits return to Denver.—*Top to bottom, CRRM; CLB; Edmunds Collection*

Denver, July 7th, 1914.

Mr. J. D. Welsh,

     General Superintendent, Denver.

Dear Sir:-

        --Division of expense C&S and D&I
        account steam trains from Eldo-
        rado Springs--

     Following is statement of expense in this

Department on account of following service:

     June 7th, engine 314, Engineer Eichman,

Conductor Scott, excursion to witness Ivy Baldwin

walking tight rope and other features at Eldorado

Springs.   This train handled C&S and D&I passengers.

Time consumed 10 hours.

        Wages of Trainmen---------$ 8.34
         "   of Enginemen---------$ 7.47
              Total------------ $15.81

     Denver & Interurban One Fourth---$ 3.95

        Yours truly,

The famed high-wire artist Ivy Baldwin lived many years at Eldorado Springs and had a steel cable installed across the canyon where he often preformed his act as seen here in 1908. The C & S and D & I ran numerous specials including those for Baldwin's performances as discussed in this letter.—*Left, CLB; Above, CRRM*

The canyon to the right in the top photo is where Ivy Baldwin did his high-wire walk and the steel cable remained in place until the early 1970s when removed to prevent would-be aerialists from attempting what might be a fatal act. The M-158 is seen at left ready to head a two-car train from the Eldorado Springs station. On May 9, 1909, L.C. McClure photographed this special inspection train at Eldorado Springs carrying stockholders and officers of a company constructing an irrigation system including a dam just west of the resort.—*Above and Below, CLB; Left, Edmunds Collection*

State University

The D & I route through Marshall reached Boulder after crossing the University of Colorado campus and running via Twelfth Street to its depot in the back of the First National Bank building at the corner of Pearl Street, where the M-155 waits about 1910. In 1918 the D & I reached an agreement with the city to leave the streets and operate directly to the C & S station. In this panoramic view the campus station is visible at the lower right of a rather open campus; today the location is in the heart of the campus.— *Right, CRRM; Below, UCWH*

Operation and Schedules on the Kite Route

From the inauguration of service until 1919, there were sixteen round trips per day between Denver and Boulder. This was cut to thirteen per day in 1920 in order to reduce the company's operating costs. Each round trip appeared on the timetable as two trains. The northbound trains bore odd numbers while the southbound trains bore even numbers. Unscheduled trains, which ran as extras, bore the number of their lead car.

Trains on the Kite route typically consisted of a single motor car or one motor car and one trailer. If holiday traffic was heavy, trains consisting of as many as six cars might be dispatched, but they always contained at least one motor car for each trailer in the train. Four trains daily in each direction carried mail. Baggage-passenger motor cars M-157 and M-158 were generally used on these runs.

Timetables varied somewhat from year to year, but 1910 was typical. The first scheduled train of the day left Boulder at 6:20 A.M., travelling to Denver via Louisville. It arrived at Interurban Loop at 7:30 A.M. The last train of the day left Denver at 11:30 P.M. travelling to Boulder via Louisville. It arrived at 12:55 A.M. Most trains left Denver on the hour and Boulder on the half hour. Throughout most of the day the routing of trains alternated between the line via Marshall and the line via Louisville. That provided passengers with a convenient opportunity for two-way travel between Boulder and those smaller communities.

The schedules allowed one hour and ten minutes, to one hour and twenty minutes for trips via Louisville. Those via Marshall were allowed one hour and twenty minutes, to one hour and twenty-five minutes. Typically twenty-five to thirty-five stops were made along the way. When operations first began, the schedules were built around one hour service between Denver and Boulder. Such schedules were impossible to keep, however. The planners assumed the motor cars would weigh fifty tons or less and thus planned on quicker acceleration. In addition, they envisioned only eight or nine stops per trip and thus significantly fewer delays.

The schedule for trains to Eldorado Springs allowed for an hour and ten minutes to an hour and twenty minutes. The time varied because of meetings with other scheduled trains.

The Denver & Interurban, operated with a staff which numbered fifty in 1926. Fifteen of the employees were trainmen, seventeen worked in car maintenance and two worked in line maintenance. The sixteen others ranged from officers to office clerks and station agents to section hands.

BOULDER

The Kite Route

TROLLEY TRIP

ELDORADO SPRINGS

75 MINUTES TO BOULDER IN THE FOOTHILLS

DENVER

Time Tables

ELECTRIC TRAINS

Between

Denver, Louisville, Marshall, Eldorado Springs and Boulder

Corrected to June 1, 1919
Subject to change without notice

The Denver & Interurban R. R.
Wm. H. EDMUNDS, Receiver

TICKET OFFICES

Denver: Interurban Station,   Phone Main 990

Boulder: Union Station,   Phone Boulder 98

Many of these employees came out of C & S service to work for the D & I. Labor agreements gave most of the trainmen dual seniority rights. These covered jobs on the Colorado & Southern's Fort Collins district as well as the D & I. Extra work and new jobs were to be offered to C & S trainmen, in the order of seniority. If none of them were interested, then new employees could be hired.

May 24, 1922   191

M D. & I., C. W. Richards, Gen'l Passenger Agt.,

IN ACCOUNT WITH

Boulder Chamber of Commerce,

Boulder, Colo.

75,000 Glacier folders		oK留
¼ cost		$1175.0

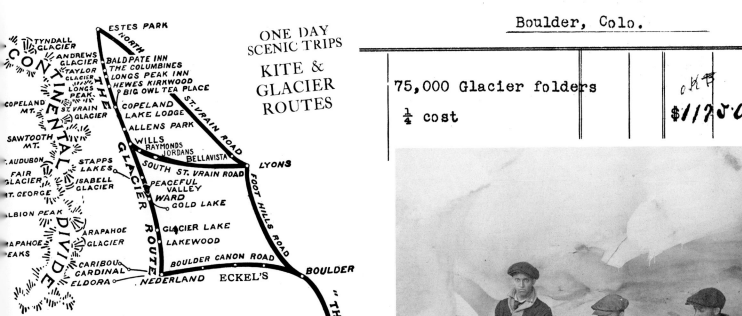

ONE DAY SCENIC TRIPS
KITE & GLACIER ROUTES

Ticket Office, Kite Route
1419 Arapahoe Street, Denver
Telephone Main 805, Branch 58

Ticket Office Glacier Route
1829 14th Street, Boulder, Colo.
Telephone Boulder 980 or 795 W

Circle Trips from Denver to Will's via Boulder Canon, the Glacier Highline and the South St. Vrain, over the Kite and Glacier Routes.

Stop over allowed at any point.   Tickets good for season.

TRIP No. 1			TRIP No. 2		
			Denver lv	8.00	a m
Denver lv	6.20	a m	Boulder ar	9.22	a m
Boulder ar	7.30	a m	Boulder lv	9.30	a m
Boulder lv	8.00	a m	Wills (dinner) ar	12.30	p m
Nederland	9.20	a m	Wills lv	1.30	p m
Glacier Lake	9.55	a m	Peaceful Valley	2.45	p m
Ward	10.35	a m	Stapps Junction	3.15	p m
Stapps Junction	10.50	a m	Ward	3.40	p m
Peaceful Valley	11.25	a m	Glacier Lake	4.20	p m
Wills (dinner) ar	12.00	noon	Nederland	4.55	p m
Wills lv	3.30	p m	Boulder ar	6.15	p m
Boulder ar	6.00	p m	Boulder lv	6.30	p m
Boulder lv	6.30	p m	Denver ar	7.50	p m
Denver ar	7.50	p m			

Extension of Trip No. 1 to Estes Park.

	Going (Read down)	Return (Read up)
Wills	12.30 p m	3.30 p m
Allens Park	12.40 p m	3.20 p m
Copeland Lake Lodge	12.55 p m	3.05 p m
Big Owl Tea Place Junct.	1.05 p m	2.55 p m
Hewes Kirkwood Junction	1.15 p m	2.45 p m
Longs Peak Inn	1.20 p m	2.40 p m
The Columbines Junction	1.20 p m	2.40 p m
Bald Pate Inn	1.33 p m	2.25 p m
Lewiston's Chalet	1.50 p m	2.10 p m
Big Thompson Hotel	1.55 p m	2.05 p m
Crags	1.58 p m	2.02 p m
Estes Park	2.00 p m	2.00 p m

Every automobile is driven by a competent, courteous, experienced mountain driver who is thoroly familiar with all the territory.

The Nederland Trip

	Going				Returning		
Station	Trip No. 1	Trip No. 2	Trip No. 3	Station	Trip No. 1	Trip No. 2	Trip No.
Boulder	8.00 a m	9.30 a m	5.30 a m	Lakewood	4.30 p m	7.30 a m	1.00 p m
Alps	8.15 a m	9.45 a m	5.45 a m	Eldora	4.30 p m	7.30 a m	1.00 p m
Boulder Falls	8.40 a m	10.10 a m	6.10 a m	Cardinal	4.30 p m	7.30 a m	1.00 p m
Eckels	8.50 a m	10.20 a m	6.20 a m	Nederland	4.55 p m	8.00 a m	1.30 p m
Tungsten	9.04 a m	10.34 a m	6.34 a m	Tungsten	5.04 p m	8.11 a m	1.45 p m
Nederland	9.15 a m	10.45 a m	6.45 a m	Eckels	5.24 p m	8.25 a m	1.59 p m
Cardinal	9.30 a m	11.00 a m	7.00 a m	Boulder Falls	5.34 p m	8.35 a m	2.09 p m
Eldora	9.35 a m	11.05 a m	7.05 a m	Alps	5.59 p m	9.00 a m	2.34 p m
Lakewood	9.30 a m	11.00 a m	7.00 a m	Boulder	6.10 p m	9.15 a m	2.45 p m

Bring overcoats and heavy wraps, as these trips lead up into the perpetual snow region, where it is often *cold.*. Ladies should also have veils and other means for protecting themselves against sunburn while among the high peaks.

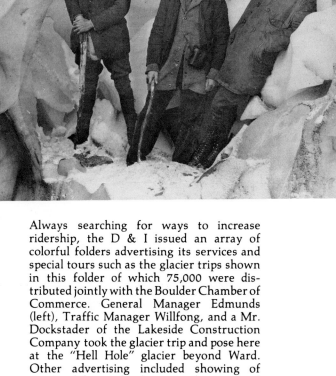

Always searching for ways to increase ridership, the D & I issued an array of colorful folders advertising its services and special tours such as the glacier trips shown in this folder of which 75,000 were distributed jointly with the Boulder Chamber of Commerce. General Manager Edmunds (left), Traffic Manager Willfong, and a Mr. Dockstader of the Lakeside Construction Company took the glacier trip and pose here at the "Hell Hole" glacier beyond Ward. Other advertising included showing of scenic slides at local movie theaters and during the mid-1920s, placement of billboards in Denver at Eleventh and Broadway, Colfax and Washington and Fifteenth and Platte streets.—*All, CRRM*

TAYLOR-BOULDER

Form 2802

THE DENVER & INTERURBAN RAILROAD COMPANY

Dec 4   1914

D I-14

Mr T. E. Fisher G. P. A.
     Building.
         Dear Sir:-

         Herewith statement of newspaper bundles handled by D & I trains, Denver to Boulder during November 1914.

     The revenue divides D & I 75% . D C T Co 25% as per letter Mr A. D. Parker Oct. 22. 1911.

The Denver Pub Co.	$77.22		D & I 75%	$137.99
The Post Ptg & Pub Co.	$94.38		DCTCo 25%	45.99
The Pueblo Chieftan.	$.37			$183.98
The Denver Express Pub Co.	$12.01			
	$183.98			

Yours truly
J. L. Bradway
Gen Aud

VOUCHERED
GENERAL PASSENGER DEPT,
D-641

While the D & I carried no freight except very minor amounts on the Eldorado Springs branch, it did make considerable revenue from hauling bundles of newspapers as indicated by this tally for the month of November 1911.—CRRM

The Denver & Interurban is not generally considered one of America's high speed electric lines but it was just that, as indicated by this speed rating in the December 1924 issue of the trade journal *Electric Traction*. The great number of stops caused it to rank only twenty-first in speed by elapsed time but when stops are excluded the D & I ranked in fifth place nationally with an average speed of 41.1 miles per hour.—CRRM

DECEMBER SPEED RANKING

ELECTRIC TRACTION'S Big Speed Contest

The following table was compiled from actual timetables and such other information as was possible to obtain. The Galveston-Houston Electric Company still retains undisputed claim for first place, while several additional roads appear in the table and some of the roads formerly shown have improved their ratings. This table will be published again with corrections and additions in the February, 1925, issue.—Editor.

NAME OF RAILWAY	RUN	Distance	Regular Stops	Time	M. P. H. including stops	Rank by elapsed time	M.P.H. not including stops*	Rank by running time
Galveston-Houston Electric Company	Galveston to Houston	50.41	6	1 hr. 15 min.	40.3	①	48.0	③
Chicago, North Shore & Milwaukee R. R.	Chicago to Milwaukee	85.5	9	2 hrs. 9 min.	39.7	②	46.5	④
††Chicago, Aurora & Elgin R. R. Co.	Chicago to Elgin	41.5	8	1 hr. 5 min.	38.3	③	50.9	①
Union Traction Co.	Muncie to Indianapolis	63.6	1	1 hr. 45 min.	36.3	④	37.0	⑫
Milwaukee Northern Railway	Milwaukee to Sheboygan	57.4	3	1 hr. 36 min.	35.9	⑤	38.2	⑩
Terre Haute, Indianapolis & Eastern	Terre Haute no Indianapolis	71.8	3	2 hrs. 5 min.	34.5	⑥	36.2	⑭
†Chicago, Lake Shore & South Bend Railway Co.	South Bend to Kensington	76.05	26	2 hrs. 15 min.	33.8	⑦	48.6	②
New York State Railways	Syracuse to Utica	48.56	2	1 hr. 28 min.	33.1	⑧	34.7	⑰
Interstate Public Service	Indianapolis to Louisville	117.02	10	3 hrs. 35 min.	32.6	⑨	36.0	⑮
Rochester and Syracuse R. R.	Rochester to Syracuse	87.0	16	2 hrs. 43 min.	32.2	⑩	40.0	⑨
Pacific Electric	Los Angeles to San Bernardino	57.78	12	1 hr. 45 min.	32.0	⑪	40.3	⑧
Illinois Traction System	Peoria to St. Louis	173.2	11	5 hrs. 25 min.	31.8	⑫	34.3	⑱
Waterloo, Cedar Falls and Northern Ry. Co.	Cedar Rapids to Waterloo	60.39	13	1 hr. 55 min.	31.5	⑬	40.7	⑥
Texas Electric	Dallas to Waco	97.19	13	3 hrs. 5 min.	31.4	⑭	36.6	⑬
The Milwaukee Electric Ry. and Light Co.	Milwaukee to Watertown	50.1	7	1 hr. 40 min.	30.6	⑮	35.0	⑯
Indianapolis and Cincinnati Traction Co.	Connersville to Indianapolis	58.2	11	1 hr. 55 min.	30.4	⑯	37.6	⑪
††Michigan Electric Railway	Grand Rapids to Kalamazoo	49.72	2	1 hr. 33 min.	29.8	⑰	33.4	⑲
Kansas City, Clay County & St. Joseph Ry. Co.	Kansas City to St. Joseph	51.3	1	1 hr. 43 min.	29.8	⑱	31.6	㉑
Lake Shore Electric	Cleveland to Toledo	120.0	18	4 hrs. 15 min.	28.2	19	32.0	⑳
**Minneapolis, Northfield & Southern Ry.	Minneapolis to Faribault	59.94	4	2 hrs. 10 min.	27.6	20	29.4	㉒
Denver & Interurban Railroad Co.	Denver to Boulder	29.5	11	1 hr. 5 min.	27.2	21	41.1	⑤
†San Francisco, Napa and Calistoga Railway	San Francisco to Calistoga	41.6	18	1 hr. 38 min.	25.5	22	40.7	⑦
Detroit United Railway	Detroit to Jackson	76.24	7	3 hrs. 8 min.	24.2	㉓	26.6	㉓
Washington-Virginia Ry. Co.	Washington to Fairfax	20.78 (See Note A)		1 hr. 18 min.	16.2	24	18.24	24

*Stops have been arbitrarily figured at two minutes each.
**Gas-Electric operation.
Note A. 56 stops, averaging 9.5 seconds each.

†A. C. operation.
††Third Rail System.

William Hillsman Edmunds
1882-1969

The history of the D & I and the working career of William Hillsman Edmunds are inseparable. It is unusual to find an instance where one man is involved with a business from construction through its lifespan and then supervises its dismantling; such was the relation of Edmunds to the D & I.

When the C & S decided to construct the D & I, they made a decision to accept the proposal of Westinghouse Electric to adopt a very new system of high voltage AC current instead of the very popular DC system developed by Thomas Edison and marketed by General Electric. In the 1890s Nikola Tesla developed the concept of alternating current and the AC induction motor. He worked for a time with Edison, but they were unable to agree and Telsa went with Westinghouse who developed his AC system. Some large AC electric installations were built in the east, but there had been no interurban application until the D & I accepted the Westinghouse bid. The company sent a team of experts to Colorado to supervise the show piece installation.

William Edmunds was born in Kentucky on October 31, 1882, studied electrical engineering at the University of Kentucky and was so interested in the wonders of the 1904 World's Fair that he landed a job as a reporter for a newspaper, writing about the electrical and mechanical displays. After the fair he went to work for Westinghouse in Pittsburgh, Pennsylvania and was selected to go to Colorado to work on the D & I installation.

In the weeks following the line's opening Edmunds and his associates checked all electrical equipment and he then accepted an offer to remain with the Denver & Interurban as general foreman. In 1912 he was promoted to electrical engineer and trainmaster and when the line went into receivership in 1918, he was appointed receiver. After successfully reorganizing the company and bringing it out of receivership, he was made general manager, a position he held until again made receiver prior to abandonment. He continued with the company as vice-president and general manager of Denver & Interurban Motor Company and after the bus operation ended he remained with Colorado & Southern and Burlington under various titles included electrical engineer-Denver and officer manager of the C & S. He retired after forty-four years of service.

To Edmunds the D & I was more than a job. He met his future wife, Ida Sherriff, on an excursion to Eldorado Springs and made his home in North Denver where he was close to the shop and offices of the railroad. He was active in his church and Masonic Lodge and became a supporter of the growing tourist business in Colorado. He made every effort to promote tours both on the D & I and later the bus company and at one time offered with several associates to purchase the motor company from the C & S. That plan failed when it was sold instead to Burlington Trailways. He is generally credited with originating the still popular slogan "Colorful Colorado." A part-time inventor, he developed and obtained a patent on the first built-in camera light meter, but was ahead of his time and found little interest in the device until years after the patent expired.

To Edmunds perhaps the high point of his career was bringing the D & I out of receivership. There were low points also; the final abandonment of the line was a great disappointment to him for he felt there was a good market for the interurban in the future. Without question, the Globeville wreck was the worst moment of his career. He arrived at the scene seven minutes after the collision and was personally devastated by the accident. It was always his belief that the difference in daylight and standard time played a part in confusing the crew and noted this in a letter many years ago during work on an article concerning the railroad.

September 29, 1947

As stated previously, our cars were operated from the city limits of Denver to the Interurban Loop and back by Denver Tramway crews as long as we operated over Tramway tracks. On the date of the wreck in question the tramway crews turned over this equipment to the D&I crew (an extra crew recruited from C&S forces for the day) at 12:18PM City Time, which was 11:18 AM by railroad time. No D&I train was due in at 12:19 PM railroad time but there was one due in at 11:18 AM and the crew figured they had nothing to clear at this point as they had the city time then in mind. From all evidences available this set of circumstances was undoubtedly the cause of the accident.

* Letter originally appeared in *Denver & Interurban* by Ira Swett.

Throughout the rest of his career Edmunds was always very concerned with the yearly time difference with the start of daylight savings time while the railroads remained on standard time.

After his retirement Edmunds remained active until his passing on April 6, 1969. His grandson, Roger, summed up his grandfather well in calling him a "futurist." He was ahead of his time with the light meter invention, his ideas to promote tourism would work better today than in his day, and he was certainly ahead of his time as he ran an electric railway which would be better suited to handling the congestion of the late twentieth century. Perhaps William Edmunds and the Kite Route were both ahead of their time.—*Edmunds Collection*

Form No. 2850—5-13-20M

BILL COLLECTIBLE.

DEPARTMENT NO. 14686

AUDIT NO. 437

DENVER, COLO. December 1st 1914 191__

The Denver & Interurban Railroad Co.,

ADDRESS __Denver, Colorado.__

} To The Colorado & Southern Railway Co. Dr.

THIS BILL MUST BE MADE IN COPYING INK AND SENT TO THE GENERAL AUDITOR FOR COPYING.

FOR proportion of wages of Dispatchers,
Agents and Operators at Joint Stations-for
the month of November 1914;

Chief Dispatcher,	$175.00	
Dispatchers(3)handling trains between		
Boulder Junction,Globeville & Semper,	450.00	
Proportion,-20%,	625.00	$125.00
Louisville, (Flat Charge)		65.00
Marshall, do		65.00
Semper(1st & 2nd Trick Operators)	$130.00	
Superior,	65.00	
Boulder,	65.00	
Louisville Junction, (2)	130.00	
Proportion,-50%,	390.00	195.00
Correct,		$450.00

IF NOT CORRECT RETURN TO J. H. BRADBURY, GENERAL AUDITOR, DENVER, COLO., WITHOUT ALTERATIONS,
AND STATE DIFFERENCES.
REMITTANCES SHOULD BE MADE TO B. F. JAMES, TREASURER, DENVER, COLO.

Since the D & I used C & S trackage and stations for much of its route, costs were proportioned between the two companies as shown in this bill from the C & S to the D & I for their share of the wages for dispatchers, station agents and operators.—*CRRM*

In these two photos we catch a glimpse of D & I officials out on the line. In the photo at left are from left to right: W.H. Edmunds, general manager; A.W. Whiteford, assistant trainmaster and C.A. Willfong, trainmaster. On the right only Edmunds, sitting on the far left, is positively identified. While the specific titles held by Edmunds, Willfong and Whiteford varied over the years they were principals of the management team throughout the history of the company.—*Both, Edmunds Collection*

The Denver & Interurban Railroad Company

Rules, Regulations and Rates of Pay Governing Motoneers and Trainmen Operating Between Globeville and Boulder and on the Eldorado Springs Branch

EFFECTIVE FEBRUARY 1, 1911

ARTICLE I.

Section 1. 34 cents per hour will be paid motoneers and conductors, and 36 cents per hour will be paid brakemen. Eight hours or less will constitute a day's work, hours to be computed consecutively from time required for duty until relieved of duty. If service is less than eight hours, motoneers, conductors and brakemen will be paid for eight hours. All time in excess of eight hours, or after completion of regular assignment, and time made by regularly assigned men outside of regular assignment, when kept in continuous service, will be paid for as overtime or mileage, whichever is the greater, but not both, in addition to pay for assigned service, at 37 cents per hour for motoneers and conductors, and 36 cents per hour for brakemen. All mileage made in excess of 5,000 miles per month will be paid for at rates of .025 cents per mile for motoneers and con-

1

ductors, and .018 cents per mile for brakemen, but such excess mileage will not be paid for in both mileage and overtime rates, but whichever rate gives the higher compensation will be paid. In computing overtime actual minutes will be paid for.

Section 2. Mileage allowance will be as follows: Between Globeville and Boulder, in either direction, 28.5 miles; round trip, 57 miles. Between Marshall and Eldorado Springs, 3.3 miles.

Section 3. Crews on the Eldorado Springs Branch will handle baggage and freight without increased compensation.

ARTICLE II.

Should time slips be sent in and all time claimed not allowed, the superintendent shall advise employes of the same, giving reasons why not allowed. In cases where there are shortages, not due to neglect or omission on the part of the employe in making out time slips, and the same are corrected and allowed, such shortages shall be paid at once, provided the amount is five dollars or over.

ARTICLE III.

When motoneers and trainmen are called and for any reason they do not go out, and are held on duty four hours ~~and thirty minutes~~, or less, they shall be paid for four hours ~~and thirty minutes~~ and stand first out; if held on duty more than four hours ~~and thirty minutes~~, they shall be allowed not less than one day's pay of eight hours and stand last out.

2

A wealth of information concerning operations and working conditions on a railroad can be determined by studying the employee's rule book. This one from the D & I is no exception.—*CRRM*

W.H. Edmunds poses with D & I employees. Edmunds was well respected and succeeded in maintaining a close knit family of D & I employees, many of whom worked for the company throughout most or all its existence.—*Edmunds Collection*

ARTICLE IV.

Crews in regular assigned service will not have their pay reduced on account of trains being annulled, except when it is necessary to suspend service on account of circumstances over which the company has no control, such as serious washouts, accidents, snow blockades and power failures, when notice has been served upon employes before coming on duty.

ARTICLE V.

Motoneers and trainmen deadheading will be paid one-half day, provided they are not deadheading to or from relief of men laying off of their own accord. No deadhead time will be allowed motoneers or trainmen deadheading on account of a new assignment.

ARTICLE VI.

Motoneers and trainmen attending court or coroner's inquest at the request of the company will be paid at the same rate they would have been entitled to had they remained on their runs; extra men not assigned will be paid nine hours each day. Legitimate expenses will be allowed when away from their home stations.

ARTICLE VII.

(a) All new runs and permanent vacancies for motoneers and trainmen on the Denver & Interurban Railroad will be bulletined on the Denver & Interurban Railroad and the Fort Collins District on the Colorado & Southern Railway for a period of five (5) days, and will be given: first, to the men holding

3

rights on the Denver & Interurban Railroad, in the order of their seniority with the Denver & Interurban Railroad; next, to employes in train and engine service on the Fort Collins District of the Colorado & Southern Railway, in the order of their rights and seniority on said district.

(b) Train and enginemen accepting employment on the Denver & Interurban Railroad take rank thereon in their respective classes from the date they qualify, and are entitled to service on the Denver & Interurban Railroad.

(c) When employes on the Denver & Interurban Railroad enter the service of the Colorado & Southern Railway they thereby forfeit their seniority on the Denver & Interurban Railroad (excepting as provided in Paragraph (d) of this Article). Such employes with Colorado & Southern rights assume those rights, and those who have no rights on the Colorado & Southern Railway take rank thereon in their respective classes from the date they qualify, and are entitled to service on the Colorado & Southern Railway.

(d) Train and enginemen accepting service on the Fort Collins District of the Colorado & Southern Railway, or on the Denver & Interurban Railroad, are required in each case to remain one year, unless a regular passenger run becomes vacant, or is created on the Colorado & Southern Railway, and should they accept such service on the Colorado & Southern Railway, they cannot return to the Denver & Interurban Railroad, unless

4

they are displaced within one year by a senior man under the provisions of the schedule, or the passenger train on which they may be employed is withdrawn, in which event they may again take service on the Denver & Interurban Railroad with rights and seniority as though they had remained in that service continuously.

(e) Season passenger runs and vacancies caused thereby not to be considered as permanent runs under this rule.

(f) Vacancies will be bulletined by superintendent of the Denver & Interurban Railroad, and applications for such vacancies will be addressed to him.

(g) Employes subject to this article who are off duty, account accidents, sickness or absence, may apply for any runs open during their absence from such cause; it being understood that such application must be made within five days of the time they report for duty.

ARTICLE VIII.

(a) Employes returned to the service of the Colorado & Southern Railway, due to reduction of force, hold their seniority on the Denver & Interurban Railroad, and when needed will be returned to the Denver & Interurban service in the order of their Denver & Interurban seniority.

(b) Employes discharged from the service of the Denver & Interurban Company for good and sufficient cause forfeit their rights with both the Colorado & Southern and Denver & Interurban Companies.

5

ARTICLE IX.

When it is known that any assigned run is to be vacant for motoneer or trainman for five days or more, the oldest man applying will be assigned to such temporary vacancy. When an assigned run is vacant for motoneer or trainman for an unknown period, an extra man may hold the run for five days, after which time the oldest man applying may take the run until the regular man returns or run is declared permanently vacant.

ARTICLE X.

Colorado & Southern employes desiring to familiarize themselves with the electric service will be given an opportunity to do so after getting permission from the proper officer of the Colorado & Southern, under such arrangements as shall be established by the proper officer of the Denver & Interurban.

ARTICLE XI.

When extra men are required the oldest available and qualified man will be called.

ARTICLE XII.

Motoneers and trainmen living within certain limits established by superintendent, when required for extra service, will be called, as nearly as practicable, one hour and thirty minutes before time to start on their runs.

ARTICLE XIII.

After continuous service of sixteen hours employes will be required to take ten hours off duty before resuming service, except in cases of washouts, wrecks or other emergencies.

6

ARTICLE XIV.

Steam trains may be run temporarily on any or all parts of the Denver & Interurban Railroad under the rates of pay and by employes of the Fort Collins District of the Colorado & Southern Railway. Steam trains permanently added on the Denver & Interurban tracks will be given to Denver & Interurban employes who are qualified, and the Colorado & Southern Railway schedules applicable to passenger service will apply.

ARTICLE XV.

A leave of absence will not be granted to exceed ninety days, except in case of sickness. Any employe absent on such leave, who does not report for duty before the expiration of that time, shall forfeit his rights.

ARTICLE XVI.

Motoneers and trainmen will not be dismissed or suspended from the company's service without just cause. In case of suspension or dismissal, if any employe thinks he has been unjustly treated, he shall have the right, within ten days, to refer his case, by written statement, to the superintendent. Within ten days after receipt of such notice his case shall be given a thorough investigation by the proper officer of the railroad company, at which he may be present, if he so desires, and also be represented by any employe of his choice. In case he shall not be satisfied with the result of said investigation he shall have the right to appeal to the general superintendent and to the general manager; in case dismissal or suspension is found to be un-

7

just, he shall be reinstated and paid for all time lost.

It is understood that in case of breach of trust, where the general officers of the company are satisfied beyond a doubt that employes are dishonest, they reserve the right to dismiss them from service without formal investigation.

Any employe, believing himself to be improperly treated under these rules and regulations, shall have the right to appeal to the general superintendent and general manager. Grievances, to be considered, must be presented within sixty days from occurrence.

ARTICLE XVII.

When employes leave the service of the company they shall be furnished a letter, signed and stamped by the superintendent, giving time of service, and in what capacity employed.

ARTICLE XVIII.

So far as it can legally do so, the Colorado & Southern Railway will transport to new place of residence family and household goods of any employe whose assignment requires such change.

ARTICLE XIX.

The Denver & Interurban Railroad Company agrees to furnish each motoneer and trainman with a copy of this schedule, free of charge.

ARTICLE XX.

The company, on its part, and the motoneers, conductors and brakemen on their part, agree with each other that they will

8

perform the several stipulations and duties as provided for in this schedule, until thirty days' notice in writing be given for change in same.

All previous agreements are hereby cancelled.

FOR THE DENVER & INTERURBAN R. R.

General Superintendent.

Approved:

President.

FOR THE COLORADO & SOUTHERN RY.

General Superintendent.

Approved:

Vice-President.

9

Denver to Boulder - Via Marshall. (2)

Notes	Station	Miles From Denver		Side Tracks
	Gorham Mine.	23+1504	23.29	
	Rockland-C.S.	23+2910	23.55	
	Marshall F.F.D.	24+1599	24.30	
	" Conn Eldorado Springs Br.	24+1650	24.31	
	Park Avenue Station	28+647	28.12	
	State University-F.F.D.	28+4761	28.81	395
11	Boulder- C.&S. Ry. Depot	29+4001	29.756	2613
	= M.P. 29.507 Via Louisville.			

Coalton to Boulder - via Louisville.

Notes	Station	Miles From Denver		Side Tracks
12	Coalton Conn Marshall Side.	16+3523	16.667	
	" F.F.D.	16+4103	16.78	
	" Conn. C.R.R. P.S.	16+4725	16.89	
	Lignite	17+2245	17.42	
	Webb. Conn. C&S Ry-P.S.	17+3388	17.64	350
	Centennial Road Crossing	18+2643	18.50	
	Louisville- F.F.D.	19+4422	19.84	672
	Hecla Road Crossing	20+2994	20.57	
	White Road Crossing	21+3331	21.63	
	Burkes Spur. P.S.	22+115	22.02	404
	Goodview Road Crossing	24+1345	24.25	392
	Weisenhorn Lake. F.F. Spr Ho.	24+5203	24.99	
	Lakeside Road Crossing	25+2754	25.52	
13	Ara Conn D.&I. Track	27+5118	27.969	262
14	Boulder-S.Line Pearl St. End D&I Track	28+2650	28.502	
	Pearl St. Conn with C&S.-P.S.	28+2762	28.523	
	" C.&S. Ry. Depot	29+2679	29.507	

Marshall to Eldorado Springs

Notes	Station	Miles From Denver		Side Tracks
15	Marshall. Conn. Eldorado Springs Br.	24+1650	24.312	
	Prudens Ranch	26+5190	26.98	
	Eldorado Springs F.F.D.	27+1709	27.32	913
	" End of Track	27+1189	27.336	1298

Denver to Boulder via Marshall (1)

Notes	Station	Miles From Denver		Side Track
1	Denver- End of Track at Subway	0+0000	0.00	722
2	" End of D.&I. Ownership 19th St.	0+915	0.173	
	" C.B.&Q. Crossing at N. 29th Ave.	0+2336	0.45	
	" Xover-between Main Lines Sa.P.S.	0+2857	0.54	
	" " No. P.S.	0+3062	0.58	
	C.B.&Q Main Freight Xing	0+3722	0.71	
	" Passing Track	0+3736	0.71	
3	" Car Barn & Passing Track	1+432	1.08	5119
	" West 38th Ave.	1+1237	1.24	
	Argo Crossing C.&S. West Side Line	1+2912	1.55	
	" Fox Street	1+4356	1.85	
	Burlington Shops	2+3942	2.75	
	DENVER-ADAMS CO. LINE	2+4382	2.85	
4	Utah Jct. & Passing Trk.	3+2332	3.44	600
	" D.L.&N.W.R.R. Xing	3+2832	3.54	
5	" Beginning D.&I. Ownership	3+2977	3.554	
	Modern Road Crossing	4+715	4.14	
	Westminster-C.S.	6+2789	6.53	504
	College Hill Road Crossing	7+3367	7.64	
	Anstees-C.S.	7+4430	7.84	502
	Crossover to C.&S. Ry. P.S.	8+111	8.02	89
6	Madison Spur-P.S.	8+141	8.05	
	ADAMS-JEFFERSON CO.LINE	8+2289	8.43	
7	Semper End of D.&I. Ownership	9+1590	9.201	
	" F.F.D.	9+2896	9.55	490
	Barzoi Road Crossing	10+1297	10.25	
	Standley Lake Road Crossing	11+2582	11.49	
	Churchs Road Crossing	12+790	17.15	
	Loraine Road Crossing	13+466	13.09	
8	JEFFERSON-BOULDER CO.LINE	14+731	14.14	
	Broomfield F.F.D.	14+861	14.16	503
	Burns Jct. Xover to C.&S. Ry. P.S.	14+4431	14.84	
	" Conn with C.B.&Q.R.R. P.S.	14+4448	14.84	
9	Coalton Conn. Line to Louisville	16+3523	16.67	335
10	" C.&S. Ry. M.L. - P.S.	16+3723	16.705	
	" Colo. R.R. P.S.	16+3804	16.72	
	" F.F.D.	16+4096	16.78	
	Superior-F.F.D.	20+555	20.11	736
	Crown-F.F.D.	22+889	22.17	
	Monarch-F.F.D.	22+3319	22.63	432

Notes

No.	
1	From M.P. 0.00 to M.P. 0.173 track is owned by D.&I.R.R.
2	From M.P. 0.173 to 3.554 track is owned by C.B.&Q.R.R. and operated by D.&I.R.R. under Contract.
3	C.B.&Q.R.R. owns to Heel of Frog of turnouts at each end of Passing track, 79.9 ft. in each case, a total of 159.8 ft.
4	C.B.&Q. Owns Passing track.
5	From M.P. 3.554 to M.P. 9.301 track is owned by D.&I.R.R., both main line and side tracks.
6	From M.P. 9.301 to M.P. 16.705 main line and sidings are owned by C.&S.Ry. and operated under lease by D.&I.R.R. Passing Track owned by C.&S.Ry.
7	" " " " " "
8	" " " " " "
9	Side tracks are at old D.&I. Jct. and are owned by C.&S.Ry.
10	From M.P. 16.705 to M.P. 29.756 main line and side tracks are owned by C.&S.Ry. and operated under trackage rights by D.&I.R.R.
11	All sidings owned by C.&S.Ry.Co.
12	From M.P. 16.667 to 27.969 main line and side tracks noted are operated under trackage rights from C.&S.Ry.
13	From M.P. 27.969 to M.P. 28.501 track is owned by D.&I.R.R. Side track at Ara is portion of C.&S.Ry. Main Line.
14	From M.P. 28.502 to M.P. 29.507 track is owned by C.&S.Ry. and operated by D.&I.R.R. under trackage rights.
15	Eldorado Branch is owned exclusively by D.&I.R.R.

January 1st-1925

SUMMARY OF MILEAGE.

MAIN LINE.

	Miles	Totals
OWNED BY D.&I.R.R.		
M.P. 0.00 to M.P. 0.173 Denver Terminals.	0.173	
M.P. 3.554 Utah. Jc. to M.P. 9.301 Semper	5.747	
M.P. 27.969 Ara to M.P. 28.501 Boulder	0.532	
Marshall to Eldorado Springs	3.026	
Total Owned Mileage		9.478
LEASED MILEAGE		
M.P. 0.173 Denver to M.P. 3.554 Utah Jc.	3.381	
M.P. 9.301 Semper to M.P. 16.705 Coalton.	7.403	
M.P. 28.502 Boulder to M.P. 28.523 Boulder	0.021	
Total Leased Mileage		10.91
JOINT MILEAGE		
M.P. 16.705 Coalton to M.P. 29.756 Boulder (via Marshall)	13.053	
M.P. 16.667 " " to M.P. 27.969 Ara (Cutoff)	11.303	
M.P. 28.523 Boulder to M.P. 29.507 Boulder "	0.584	
Total Joint Mileage		25.340
Total Operated Mileage		45.628

SIDE TRACKS

Location	Owned	Leased	Joint	Totals	Miles
Denver to Utah Jct.	5741	760		6501	1.23
Utah Jct. to Semper	1095			1095	0.21
Semper to Coalton.		1328		1328	0.25
Coalton to Boulder		398	3778	4176	0.79
" " Ara (Cutoff)			2080	2080	0.40
Eldorado Springs Branch	2211			2211	0.42
Totals	9047	2486	5858	17391	3.30
Miles	1.72	0.47	1.11	3.30	

A typical scene at the new shop with cars awaiting their assignments. Since these cars have not yet been converted to double ended operation the photo was likely taken in 1923, shortly after the end of street operations.—*UCWH*

Denver & Interurban Operations
The Cars, the Shops and the Power System

Interurban Cars

The cars of the Denver & Interurban bore the distinctive mark of the steam railroaders who bought them. The cars were almost as large and as heavy as railroad coaches. They were ten feet wide, rather than the interurban standard of eight to nine feet. They had sheet metal roofs and steel frames as opposed to the canvas and wood favored by most trolley lines, and they were powered by alternating current at 11,000 volts. That current supply had previously become the choice of the New Haven Railway and the Norfolk & Western Railway. It later was also chosen by the Pennsylvania Railroad. In order to make the D & I cars operable on street railway trackage, they contained a unique dual current electrical system which could also run on 550 volts DC. Because of their size and solid construction, these cars looked right at home on the Colorado & Southern. On urban streets, however, they seemed huge.

In January 1908, the St. Louis Car Company received an order for eight motor cars and four trailers. All were delivered in June. Six of the motor cars, M-151 through M-156, were straight passenger cars. Two, M-157 and M-158 were baggage-passenger combinations. These eight were fifty-five feet six inches long and cost roughly $21,000.00 each. The trailers were straight passenger cars, numbered 201 through 204, and cost roughly $6,000.00 each. They were fifty-three feet ten inches long.

Interiors of the cars were finished in mahogany, and the seats were covered with dark green imitation leather. Seating capacities were fifty-nine for the passenger cars, fifty-eight for the trailers, and forty-six for the baggage-passenger combinations. Electrical equipment was provided by Westinghouse. The D & I motor cars were equipped with four AC/DC, 125 horsepower traction motors. These provided enough power for trains consisting of one motor car and one trailer to ascend a two percent grade and to cruise at fifty miles per hour. Controls for the cars were located

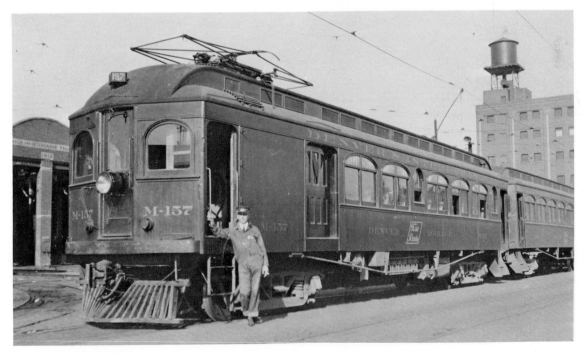

Fred Neff, a Denver Tramway motorman, poses with the M-157 and a trailer in front of the original shops at Twenty-third and Market streets in 1921, about one year before the D & I moved to the new shop and ended all operation over the Tramway's line.—*Sam Wheeler Photo, CRRM*

only in the front ends of motor cars, but plug-in multiple unit control systems allowed the operation of several cars as a single train. Pantographs were used for AC current collection and trolley poles for DC.

The cars were painted Pullman green with gold trim and rode on ALCO type A trucks. These trucks had thirty-eight-inch wheels and were designed to carry heavy loads. The motor cars weighed sixty-two and one-half tons each while the trailers weighed thirty-three tons. These car weights were quite high when compared to interurbans of the Denver Tramway. Their motor cars Nos. 20 through 25, which were built in 1909, weighed only twenty-four tons each.

Between 1908 and 1926, the D & I cars received a number of modifications.

In 1910, a snow plow and flanger were built for the M-154 to allow its use in bucking winter snow drifts. Also, in that year, the Denver Tramway was allowed to rewind all of the D & I traction motors to lower their current consumption. According to the Tramway, D & I cars had been using excessive amounts of current on the Tramway line. Little is known regarding whether this remedy was totally successful, but it could have been money spent for nothing. The motor changes caused the cars to run slower as well as reducing their current consumption. The response of motormen was to notch out their controllers and motor the cars longer and harder in order to meet schedules. This may have eliminated any reduction in current use and, in addition, it overheated the traction motors. The problems were especially severe when trailers were being pulled, and soon traction motors began to burn out. After losing nine motors to this fate, the D & I equipped its cars with traction motor blowers. The forced-air ventilation allowed the motors to put out thirty percent more horsepower without overheating. This made it safe once again for motormen to run fast. The blowers were installed in 1911, as were slack adjusters which automatically took the slack out of linkages in the brake system.

In 1920, the D & I began changing the gear ratio on its cars from 2.6:1 to 3.3:1. This reduced the power demand by making the cars run at lower speeds and accelerate more effortlessly. This change was required by an electric power rate reduction agreement which was worked out with Western Light & Power Company. The work was completed in 1922.

On Labor Day 1920, M-153 and M-158 collided head on at Globeville. Due to the severity of the damage, M-153 was declared a total loss and M-158 was out of service for four years. The electrical equipment from M-153 was used to convert trailer No. 201 into a motor car which was then renumbered M-159. Other parts of M-153 were used in rebuilding M-158. In 1924, the M-158 and M-159 re-entered service and the stripped hulk of M-153 was scrapped.

During 1923 and 1924, the D & I performed most of the work to double end all of its cars. This was to allow for efficient service into Union Station. The work involved removing one and one-half tons of assorted direct-current equipment, installing passenger steps on the front ends and control equipment on the rear ends. Boiler tube pilots on both ends replaced the old wooded pilots which had previously been only on the fronts. Headlights were also installed on both ends. A company memo dated October 12, 1925, stated that the double ending work was ninety-one percent complete. It did not, however, detail what the remaining nine percent was. Shop crews performed all of this work between regular maintenance jobs and it progressed slowly.

Six Denver & Interurban cars await shipment from the St. Louis Car Company in spring 1908. From left to right are cars M153, M154 and M-155. This photo and an accompanying story were featured in the *Electric Railway Journal* describing the newly completed D & I.—*CRRM*

Trailer 201 has been spotted for its builder's photo at the St. Louis Car Company in March 1908.—
CRRM

The M-158 is seen in 1908 at the builder and again less than twenty years later on July 18, 1927 while in storage after abandonment. It would never run again but soon be burned to salvage the scrap metal. After the M-158 was wrecked at Globeville it was rebuilt with a smaller baggage section as seen in comparing these two photos.—*Above, CRRM; Below, DPL*

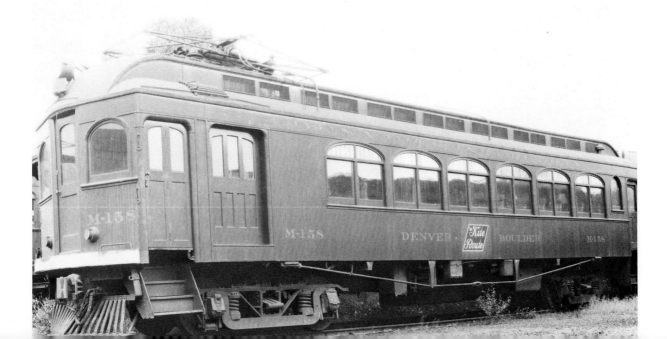

 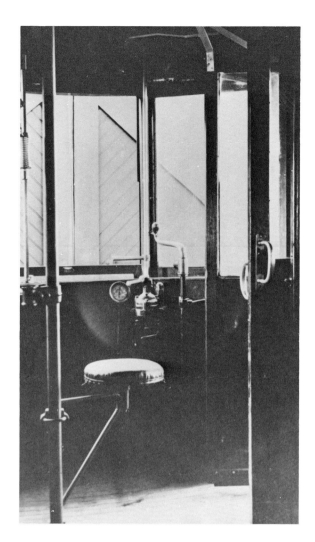

Very few interior views of D & I cars are known to exist but these photos provide a rare glimpse inside. Above can be seen the engineer's compartment—for a time the D & I used the unique term "Motoneers," but they were often simply called motormen by the public. Below and at the left on the opposite page are views of the back vestibule of the M-157. At the far right is the only known photo of the passenger compartment of a D & I car. The seats are large and comfortable with good lighting and handy overhead baggage racks. An Ohmer Fare Register is visible at the end of the car and a bill for rental of the fare registers appears at the lower right.—*Above and Far Right, Edmunds Collection; Others, CRRM*

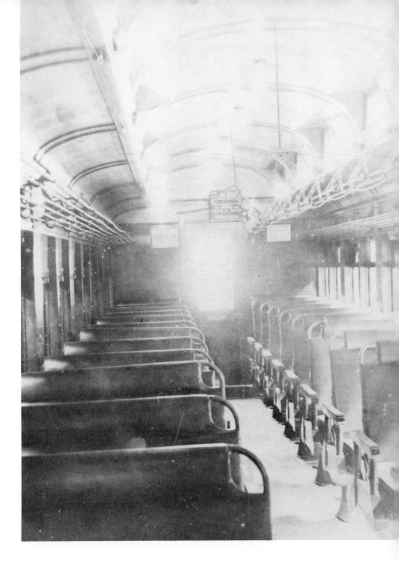

John F. Ohmer,
President & Genl. Mgr.

E. Frank Brewster,
Vice President.

W. B. Farnham,
Treasurer.

J. H. Stedman,
Secretary.

CAPITAL STOCK $1,500,000.

399

Ohmer Fare Register Company.

of Dayton, Ohio.

CABLE ADDRESS OHMEREGISTER
WESTERN UNION CODE USED

Dayton, Ohio. NOV 2 0 1914 191

The Denver & Interurban R. R. Co.,

Denver, Colo.

To Rental	8	Registers for Month of	Nov.	30 ds.	a	.80	24	00	
	12		"	30 ds.	a	2.88	86	40	110.40
									5 52
				less 5%					$104.88

82.08

228

104.88

APPROVED
W H Edmunds
Elec. Engr. & Trainmaster.

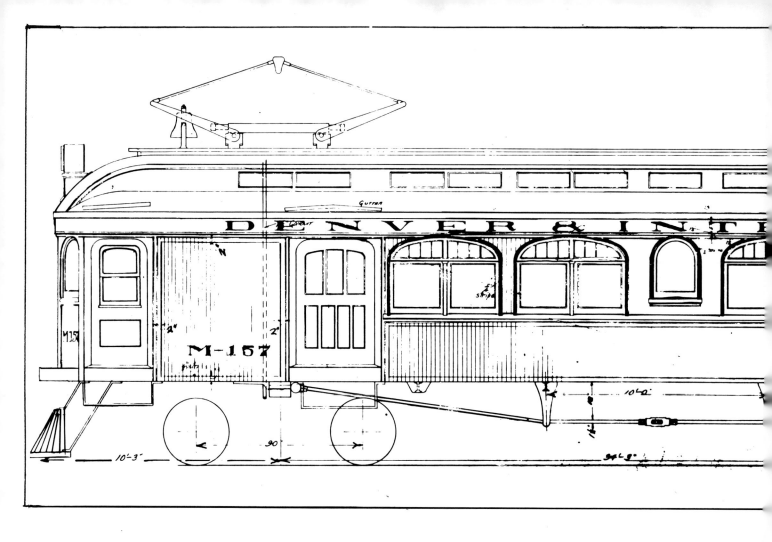

FORM P.B 39

NO CLAIMS OWED UNLESS MADE WITHIN 10 DAYS FROM RECEIPT OF THIS INVOICE

ELECTRIC SERVICE SUPPLIES CO.

MANUFACTURERS, JOBBERS, EXPORTERS

RAILWAY MATERIAL ELECTRICAL SUPPLIES

MONADNOCK BUILDING

RECEIVED

CHICAGO   OCT. 13-1922

Delivery F. O. B. ....

Price Checked ....
For Purchasing A

BILL NO.	1019-33	
OUR ORDER	122590	SOLD TO
AGENT	12-D	
BUYER'S ORDER	21-40	
DEPT. REQ.	F-9-211	SHIPPED TO
SHIPPED VIA.	P&R-B&O-CB&Q	

SOLD TO   DENVER & INTERURBAN RD. CO.
                      DENVER - COLORADO

SHIPPED TO   SAME ℅ STKPR
                      23RD & MARKET ST.

F.O.B.   FACTORY   PACKED IN   3 BBLS 225#   TERMS: NET CASH 30 DAYS

6	NO. 19543 NO- T-128 GOLDEN GLOW HEADLIGHTS WITH 5 FT. LEADS & PLUGS			
		53.50 EACH	321	00
	LESS 50%			
NO CASH DISCOUNT	MEMO B/L ATTACHED		160	50

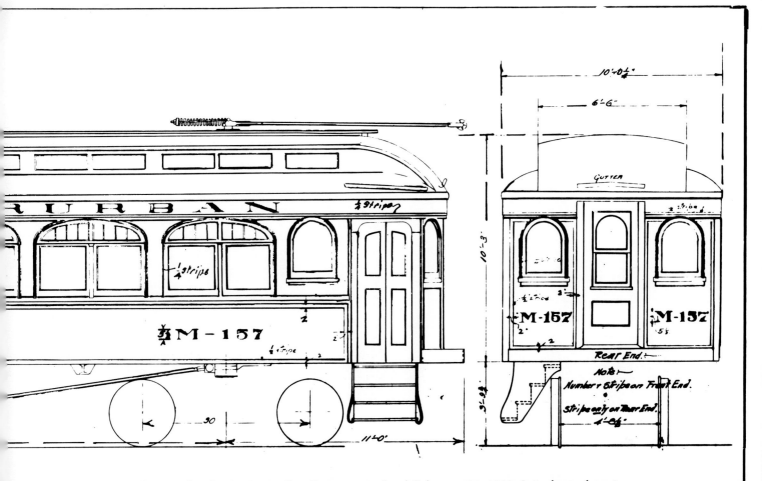

This drawing by the St. Louis Car Company is dated February 20, 1908. It is shown here in approximately 0-gauge scale. In 1922 the D & I began to prepare their cars for double end operation to avoid the need to wye them at Denver's Union Station. Additional bells and headlights were required for double end operation as reflected in the order for headlights to the Electric Service Supplies Company.—*All, CRRM*

Denver Boulder Division		DENVER & INTERURBAN	
		Motor Cars M-151 to M-158	
Trucks - American Loco. Co. Type A	Card 873 C	Pantograph Valve Magnets 2	Type 386-0
Axles - Bettendorf 6½ Dia. 7¾ Gear Seat		Master Controller 1	334-A
Wheels	38" Steel Tired	Control Junction Boxes 3	426
Brake Shoes	Castg. G-1993	Control Batteries 2	3-RI
Journal Boxes Franklin N.3 Card 173-E-3090		Train Line Receptacle 4	448
Journal Brass	5½ X10"	Train Line Jumper 1	449
Axle Brass	6½ X12½ Patt. Q.B.105-106	Lightning Arrester 1	Westg. Type 'MP'
Gear Ratio	Gear 66 - Pinion 25	Headlight	Crouse Hinds Imperial
		Pneumatic Lubricator 1	Emery P-4
Motors 4-Westg. 148-A 125 HP AC-DC.		Resistance Q3 Motor	S-310082
Compressor Motor Q3-7½ HP AC-DC.		Resistance XB2.5 Motor	S-416826
Blower Motor XB-25. 5 HP AC-DC.		Heaters M-151 to M-156 Consolidated, 2 Series 12	
Motor Generator ⅙ HP Style 82486		Heaters M-157 & M-158 Consolidated, 2 Series 10	
Transformer - 250 KW. 015.C. 1000-636 V.		Brake Valve	W.A.B. Form M-15-C
Preventive Coils 2-156 V-137.5 Amp. S.303502		Triple Valve	W.A.B. Form L-3
Preventive Coils 1-78 V- 275 Amp. S.331955		Feed Valve Pc. 11929. W.A.B. Form B-3	
Switch Group 1-AC Voltage Type 251-K		Duplex Air Gauge W.A.B. 3½ Pc. 12350	
Switch Group 1 Motor Feed Type 251-J2		Car Seats	St. Louis Car Co.
Line Switch 11000 V. oil break Type 304-C		Hand Brakes	N.B.Co. Peacock
Line Switch 550 V. DC. Type 301-J		Sanders	O.B.Co.
Blower Motor Switch AC-DC. Type 505-C		Gong	Overhead 14"
Field Switch Type 176-F-3		Whistle	14" Trombone
Reverser Switch Type 176-C		Blower Fan	15" Sirocco
Change Over Switch Type 358		Register	Ohmer
Reldy 550 V. DC Type 389		Brake Hose 1"X22" F.P.4 Coupler 1x1 Nipple	
Relay 300 V. AC. Type 388		Control Hose ¾ X 22" E.P.3 Coupler ¾ x ¾ Nipple	
Pump Governor Westinghouse Type J		Reservoir Main 2	16" X48"
Trolley 11000 V. Pantograph U.S. N. 111-A		Reservoir Aux. 1	14" X 33"
Trolley 550 V. DC. U.S. N. 6		Reservoir Emergency 1	14" X 33"
Trolley Pole 10-10½ - 1¾ X 1" O.D.		Reservoir Whistle 1	16" X 33"
Trolley Harp U.S. Form 12			
Trolley Wheel 6" G.E. N. 17			
Retriever Earll N. 5			
Grid Diverters 7 Frames 8" 3-Pt.			

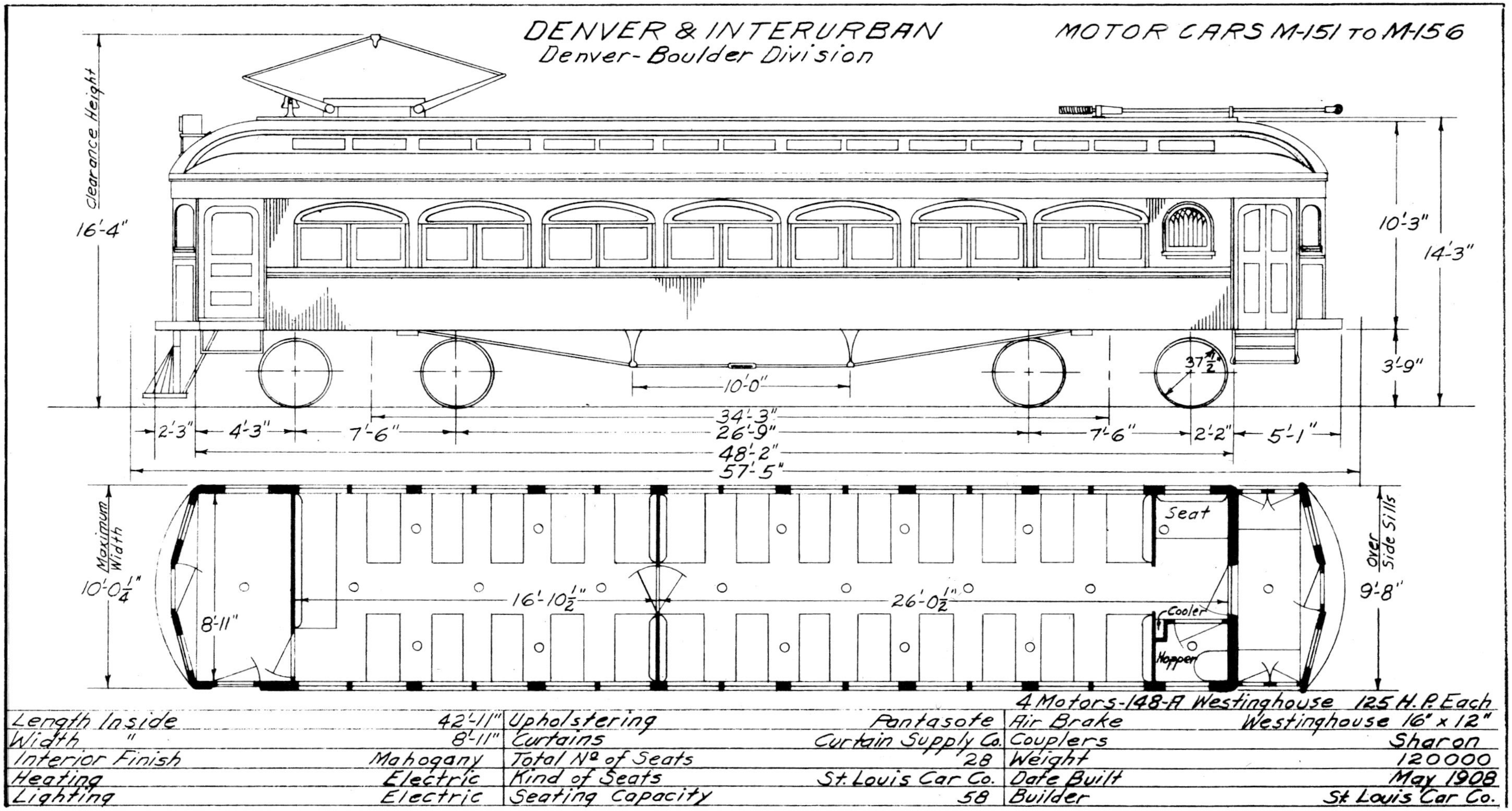

DENVER & INTERURBAN
Denver-Boulder Division
MOTOR CARS M-151 TO M-156
Clearance Height 16'-4"
10'-3"
14'-3"
3'-9"
37½"
10'-0"
2'-3"
4'-3"
7'-6"
34'-3"
26'-9"
7'-6"
2'-2"
5'-1"
48'-2"
57'-5"
Maximum Width 10'-0¼"
8'-11"
16'-10½"
26'-0½"
Seat
Cooler
Hopper
Over Side Sills 9'-8"
4 Motors-148-A Westinghouse 125 H.P. Each
Length Inside 42'-11"
Width " 8'-11"
Interior Finish Mahogany
Heating Electric
Lighting Electric
Upholstering Pantasote
Curtains Curtain Supply Co.
Total No. of Seats 28
Kind of Seats St. Louis Car Co.
Seating Capacity 58
Air Brake Westinghouse 16" x 12"
Couplers Sharon
Weight 120000
Date Built May 1908
Builder St Louis Car Co.

—Drawing by F. Hol Wagner

This drawing is in HO-gauge scale.

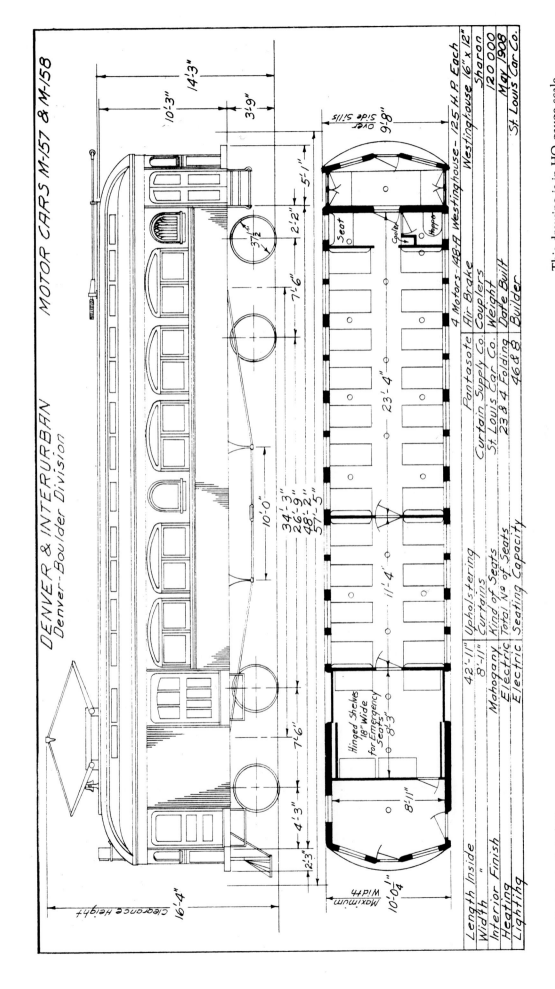

DENVER & INTERURBAN
Denver-Boulder Division

MOTOR CARS M-157 & M-158

Length Inside	42'-11"	Upholstering	Pantasote
Width	8'-11"	Curtains	Curtain Supply Co.
Interior Finish	Mahogany	Kind of Seats	St. Louis Car Co.
Heating	Electric	Total Nº of Seats	23 & 4 Folding
Lighting	Electric	Seating Capacity	46 & 8

		Air Brake	Westinghouse
4 Motors	48-A Westinghouse - 125 H.P. Each	Couplers	Sharon
		Weight	120,000
		Date Built	May 1908
Westinghouse 16" x 12"		Builder	St. Louis Car Co.

This drawing is in HO-gauge scale.

—Drawing by F. Hol Wagner

75

ROSTER OF
DENVER & INTERURBAN RAILROAD EQUIPMENT

THE DENVER-BOULDER KITE ROUTE

NUMBER	TYPE	SEAT CAPTY	BUILDER	BUILT	LENGTH	WEIGHT	MOTORS	REMARKS
M-151	Pass Motor	58	St. Louis	5-08	55'6"	120,000	4, WH 125 hp	
M-152	Pass Motor	58	St. Louis	5-08	55'6"	120,000	4, WH 125 hp	
M-153	Pass Motor	58	St. Louis	5-08	55'6"	120,000	4, WH 125 hp	Wrecked 1920, Scrapped 1924 Electrical equipment to #201
M-154	Pass Motor	58	St. Louis	5-08	55'6"	120,000	4, WH 125 hp	
M-155	Pass Motor	58	St. Louis	5-08	55'6"	120,000	4, WH 125 hp	
M-156	Pass Motor	58	St. Louis	5-08	55'6"	120,000	4, WH 125 hp	
M-157	Bag/Pass Motor	46	St. Louis	5-08	55'6"	120,000	4, WH 125 hp	
M-158	Bag/Pass Motor	46	St. Louis	5-08	55'6"	120,000	4, WH 125 hp	Wrecked 1920 Out of service 1920–1924
M-159	Pass Motor	59	St. Louis	5-08	53'10"	120,000	4, WH 125 hp	Ex-201, entered service 1924
201	Pass Trailer	59	St. Louis	5-08	53'10"	66,750	None	Removed from service 5/21 for conversion to M-159
202	Pass Trailer	59	St. Louis	5-08	53'10"	66,750	None	
203	Pass Trailer	59	St. Louis	5-08	53'10"	66,750	None	
204	Pass Trailer	59	St. Louis	5-08	53'10"	66,750	None	
403	Pass Trailer	56	Pullman	1887	61'2"	61,000	None	Rebuilt for D&I Service 1909, Ex C&S #403
404	Pass Trailer	56	Osgood & Bradley	1885	61'2"	61,000	None	Rebuilt for D&I Service 1909, Ex-C&S #404
01	Line Car	None	D & I	1909	36'2"		None	Built on Ex-C&S flat car #843
101	Flat Car	None			35'		None	Ex-C&S flat car 11511 purchased in 1923

All Kite route rolling stock sold at auction on 2/16/27 to Denver Metal & Machinery Co.

This HO-gauge operating model of M-159 was built by Noel Holley for use on the trolley line of the Denver HO Club layout at the Colorado Railroad Museum in Golden. The car is not an exact replica but aroused Noel's interest in the D & I, leading eventually to his co-authoring of this book. The catenary and pole line construction drawings at right may also be of interest to modelers.—Both, *Noel Holley*

DENVER & INTERURBAN RY

CATENARY AND
POLE LINE CONSTRUCTION

11,000 volts AC

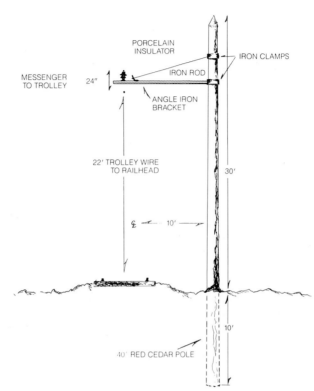

PORCELAIN
INSULATOR

IRON CLAMPS

MESSENGER
TO TROLLEY

24"

IRON ROD

ANGLE IRON
BRACKET

22' TROLLEY WIRE
TO RAILHEAD

30'

℄ — 10'

10'

40' RED CEDAR POLE

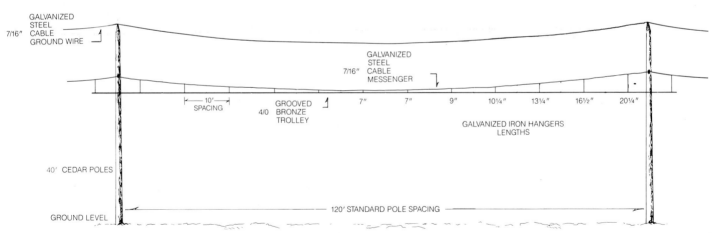

GALVANIZED
STEEL
7/16" CABLE
GROUND WIRE

GALVANIZED
STEEL
7/16" CABLE
MESSENGER

10'
SPACING

4/0
GROOVED
BRONZE
TROLLEY

7"   7"   9"   10¼"   13¼"   16½"   20¼"

GALVANIZED IRON HANGERS
LENGTHS

40' CEDAR POLES

GROUND LEVEL

120' STANDARD POLE SPACING

(Not to scale)

TRACK CURVATURE (in degrees)	POLE SPACING
None	120'
1	120'
2	110'
3	90'
4	80'
5	70'
6	60'
7	50'
8	50'
9	50'
10	50'

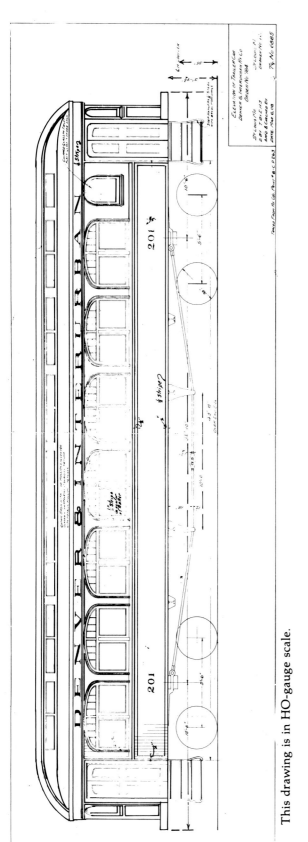

This drawing is in HO-gauge scale.

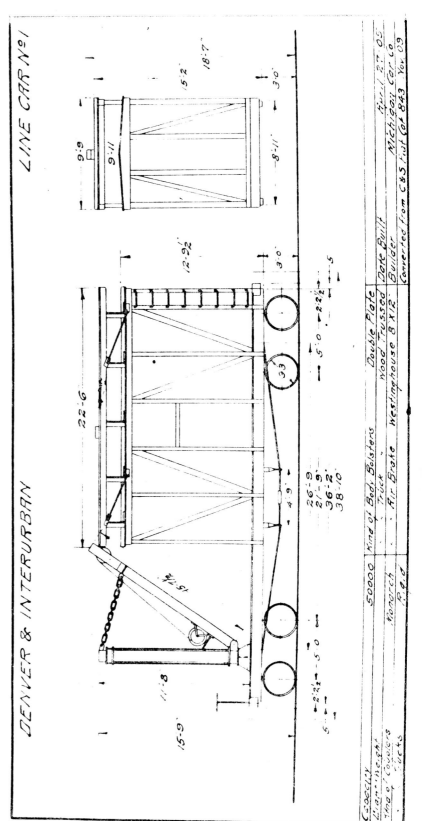

Additional Kite Route
Rolling Stock

In 1909, it became apparent that more rolling stock was needed to meet peak service requirements. In order to allow the D & I to postpone the purchase of additional new equipment, the C & S loaned it two obsolete coaches. The No. 403 had been built by Pullman in 1887, and No. 404 by Osgood & Bradley in 1885. Both were open platform sixty-one-footers. At a cost of $1,257.00 the D & I equipped these cars with rounded platform extensions and MCB radial couplers. This allowed the cars to be towed around the tight radius curves in city streets. The cars remained in interurban service permanently and were purchased by the D & I in 1921. Due to their age, however, the cars had little market value, and the D & I acquired No. 403 for $835.00 and No. 404 for $696.00.

In 1909, the D & I also found it had need for a tool car with a light derrick on it. To meet this need, thirty-six-foot C & S flat car No. 843 was purchased and converted into D & I No. 1. It was used as a line work car.

A second flat car was purchased in 1923 for materials handling. This was C & S No. 11511, a 35-foot car with a 50,000-pound capacity. The C & S had previously condemned it as unsuitable for freight service. This car became D & I No. 101.

During its eighteen year existence, the D & I owned an assortment of gasoline powered inspection cars and section cars used by line and track maintenance crews. In 1926, six of these were on the roster.

The D & I never owned any locomotives or freight cars. When members of the public critized the cash poor line for failing to seek revenues from freight hauling, the reason given for not pursuing this business was that the Tramway was unwilling to permit freight trains on its tracks. Company documents, however, reveal the real reason to be a verbal prohibition by the Burlington and the Colorado & Southern. The parent companies did not believe that D & I could generate new freight business and did not want it to siphon off existing C & S business.

—*Equipment drawings and data,- CRRM*

Fort Collins Street Railway Cars

In August 1907, the D & I bought four, thirty-eight-foot wooden streetcars from the Woeber Car Company. In January 1908, four, forty-one-foot cars were purchased from the Jewett Company. All eight cars were Brewster green, with oak interiors, cane seats, and rode on Baldwin trucks. These similar appearing cars operated on 550-volt direct current and were used only in Fort Collins. The Woeber cars seated forty and were numbered M-101 through M-104. The Jewett Cars seated forty-four and were numbered M-105, M-106, 107 and 108. The two trailers were identical to the motor cars, but carried no motors. The street railway line began operation on January 1, 1908, and was shut down by the D & I on July 10, 1918. The only significant modification to this group of cars resulted from a wreck in 1915. The M-102 sideswiped a steam shovel and suffered such extensive damage to its wooden body that it was scrapped. The electrical equipment from the wrecked car was installed on the 107. That car thus became the M-107. In 1918, the M-105, M-106 and M-107 were sold to the Oklahoma Railway and were renumbered 94, 95 and 96.

Equipment Data	
Ft. Collins Division Motor Cars M-101 To M-106	
Trucks	Baldwin Class 72-22
Axle	5½ Dia. 6" Gear Seat
Journals	4¼ X 8
Journal Box	30 Ton MCB Franklin No 3
Wheels	33" Std. Freight Car Cast Iron
Motors	4 G.E. 80 40HP 500 V.
Gear Ratio	Gear 67. Pinion 19
Controller 2	K-28
Compressor 1	CP-21
Governor	G.E. Type M-C Form B
Circuit Breaker 2	MR-5
Trolley Base	U.S. No 2
Trolley Pole	U.S. 12'
Trolley Harp	Bayonet
Trolley Wheel	4" New Haven
Lightning Arrester	2 G.E. Electrolitic
Brake Valve	2 G.E. Type S Form C
Heaters	Consolidated, 2 Series of 8
Seats	Hale & Kilburn
Retriever	Earll No 4
Hand Brake M-101 to M-104	Ratchet
Hand Brake M-105 To M-108	Jewett
Car Body Plan M-101 To M-104	Woeber
Car Body Plan M-105 To M-108	Jewett C170 33
Register	Ohmer

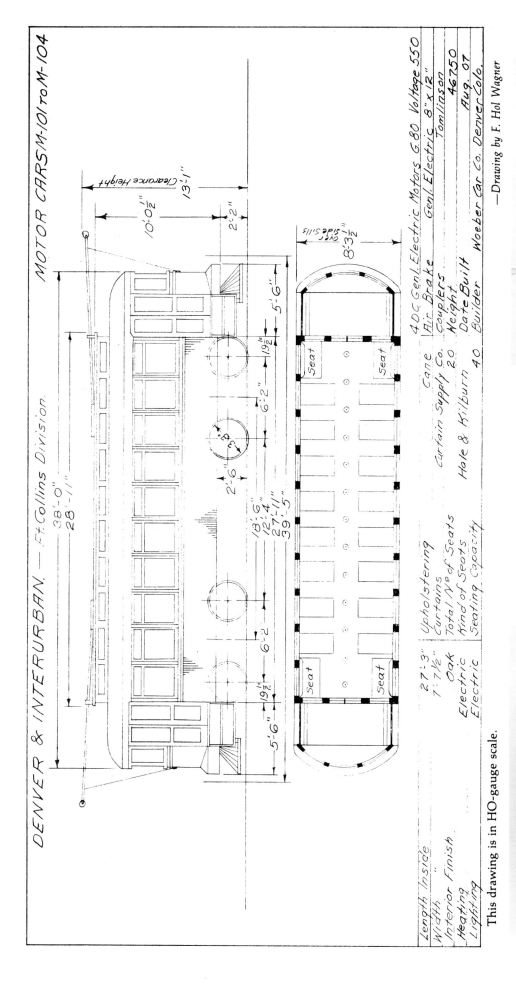

DENVER & INTERURBAN. — Ft. Collins Division.

MOTOR CARS M-101 to M-104

13'-1" — Clearance Height
10'-0½"
2'-2"
38'-0"
28'-11"
5'-6"   19½"   6'-2"   2'-6"   3'-8½"   6'-2"   19½"   5'-6"
18'-6"
12'-4"
27'-11"
39'-5"
over sills 51½"
8'-3½"

Seat

Length Inside	27'-3"
Width	7'-7½"
Interior Finish	Oak
Heating	Electric
Lighting	Electric
Upholstering	Cane
Curtains	Curtain Supply Co.
Total N° of Seats	20
Kind of Seats	Hale & Kilburn
Seating Capacity	40

	4 DC Genl. Electric Motors G 80 Voltage 550
Air Brake	Genl. Electric 8"x 12"
Couplers	Tomlinson
Weight	46750
Date Built	Aug. 07
Builder	Woeber Car Co. Denver Colo.

This drawing is in HO-gauge scale.

—Drawing by F. Hol Wagner

M-102 is seen in late 1907 as it is ready to be unloaded, and M-10'6 was photographed shortly after entering service.—Both, CRRM

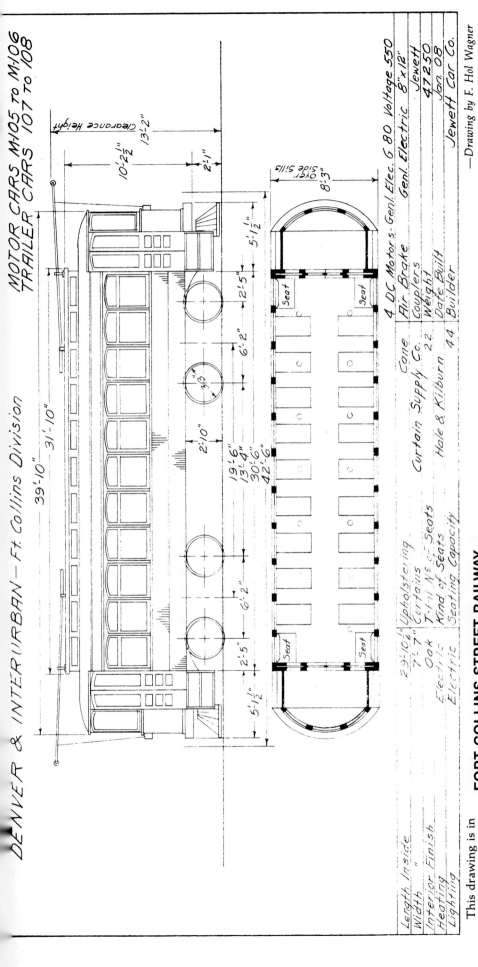

MOTOR CARS M-105 to M-106
TRAILER CARS 107 to 108

DENVER & INTERURBAN—Ft. Collins Division

Clearance Height
13'-2"
10'-2½"
2'-1"

39'-10"
31'-10"

over Side Sills
8'-3"

5'-1½"
2'-5"
6'-2"
3'-3"
2'-10"
19'-6"
13'-4"
30'-6"
42'-6"
6'-2"
2'-5"
5'-1½"

Seat

Length Inside	29'-0½"	Upholstering
Width	"	7'-7"	Curtains
Interior Finish	Oak	Total No. of Seats
Heating	Electric	Kind of Seats
Lighting	Electric	Seating Capacity

Cane	4 DC Motors	Genl. Elec. G.80 Voltage 550
Curtain Supply Co.	Air Brake	Genl. Electric 8"x12"
22	Couplers	Jewett
Hale & Kilburn	Weight	47,250
44	Date Built	Jan. 08
	Builder	Jewett Car Co.

—Drawing by F. Hol Wagner

This drawing is in HO-gauge scale.

FORT COLLINS STREET RAILWAY

NUMBER	TYPE	SEAT CAPTY	BUILDER	BUILT	OVERALL LENGTH	WEIGHT	MOTORS	REMARKS
M-101	Pass Motor	40	Woeber	8-07	39'5"	46,750	4, GE 40 hp	Scrapped 1919
M-102	Pass Motor	40	Woeber	8-07	39'5"	46,750	4, GE 40 hp	Wrecked, total loss 1915, Motors to #107
M-103	Pass Motor	40	Woeber	8-07	39'5"	46,750	4, GE 40 hp	Scrapped 1919
M-104	Pass Motor	40	Woeber	8-07	39'5"	46,750	4, GE 40 hp	Scrapped 1919
M-105	Pass Motor	44	Jewett	1-08	42'6"	47,250	4, GE 40 hp	Sold to Oklahoma Ry as #94, 1918
M-106	Pass Motor	44	Jewett	1-08	42'6"	47,250	4, GE 40 hp	Sold to Oklahoma Ry as #95, 1918
M-107	Pass Motor	44	Jewett	1-08	42'6"	47,250	4, GE 40 hp	Sold to Oklahoma Ry as #96, 1918
107	Trailer	44	Jewett	1-08	42'6"	32,500	None	Motorized approx. 1915 became M-107
108	Trailer	44	Jewett	1-08	42'6"	32,500	None	Scrapped 1919

81

Interurban Shops

The first D & I shop was built in 1909 in a wholesale food and warehouse area near Denver's central business district. It was located on the Tramway route at Twenty-third and Market Street. The shop was a large 130-foot by 130-foot brick structure containing six tracks, inspection pits and repair facilities capable of performing heavy work. A two-story wing extended forty feet beyond the front of the carbarn and provided office space. The building had enough indoor storage space for twelve cars. Additional car storage tracks were located outside. The D & I's single-ended cars could be turned on the wye in front of the shop, so this building served as the Denver terminal when Tramway strikes closed Interurban Loop. This shop was closed in September 1922 and put up for sale. The Denver & Interurban needed a shop which could be reached without the use of street trackage and direct current power. Since the company was cash short, the plan was to raise money for a new shop by selling the old one. Unexpectedly, no buyer was found for the old building. Prospective purchasers felt that the building would require costly alterations in order to make it suitable for any commercial business. The building was sold to the C & S in 1927 and to a private purchaser in 1928. It was later destroyed by fire.

The need for a new shop first became apparent in 1917, when the D & I began considering the use of Union Station as a terminal. After much study the D & I decided to locate its new shop at Thirty-sixth and Fox streets, next to the Burlington's line. Approval to construct a new building was granted in 1921. The selected design was a general purpose industrial building which could be constructed from a commercially available standard plan. The plan required minimal modification in order to serve as an interurban shop. Architectural work and construction were begun in May 1922 and took only sixty days to finish. The building had brick walls, a concrete floor and a steel truss roof. The main portion of the building was 49 feet by 183 feet and contained three repair tracks.

Twenty feet above the rails of one track was an 11,000-volt trolley wire used for electrical tests. Adjoining the building on its south side were two side bays, each twenty-two feet by five inches wide. The near bay contained offices, a store room and a machine shop, while the second bay contained a paint shop with a one-car capacity. Car storage at this location was on outdoor yard tracks. Following the abandonment of interurban service, this became the Denver & Interurban Motor Company bus barn. It was later sold to the Quick-Way Truck Shovel Company and used until 1948 when it was torn down to make way for construction of Denver's Valley Highway.

Denver and Interurban Railway Co. 1908 proclaims the sign above the M-153 in this 1910 photo of the original D & I shop and barn on the northwest corner of Twenty-third and Market streets in downtown Denver. The arrangement of this well-equipped facility is seen on the floor plan.— *Both, CRRM*

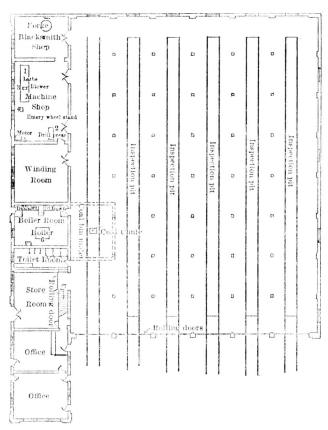

The original D & I shops are seen in these two photos soon after completion. The car to the right of the shop is very likely one of the two coaches obtained from the C & S and converted by the D & I to use as trailers.—*Above, CRRM; Below, Edmunds Collection*

Denver Tramway motorman Sam Wheeler looks from the cab of M-155, ready to take the big interurban on its run through the city to the end of the Tramway's Globeville line where a D & I crew will take over. Sam Wheeler and a few other Tramway men preferred this special assignment over regular Tramway runs.—*CRRM*

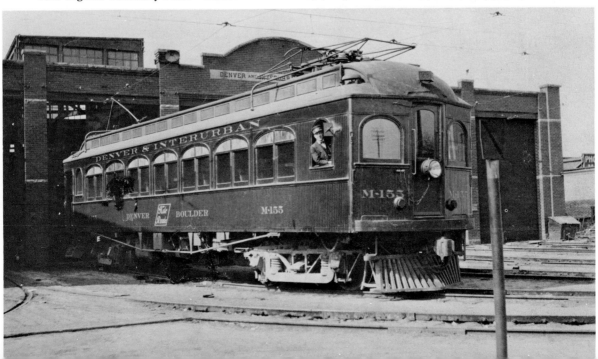

DENVER, COLO. *Jan 16* 191*5*

Denver & Interurb Ry Co.

City

GENERAL WATCH INSPECTOR C. & S. RY.

" " " DENVER & INT. R. R.

" " " C. & W.

" " " D. B. & WESTERN

" " " C. & S. E. RY.

LOCAL WATCH INSPECTOR A. T. & S. FE

Jan 16 To Repairing Seth & Thomas Regulator #34019 Clg, Cushing & demagnetized 2 au

2 au

The D & I maintained a standard clock at the shop and when that faithful Seth Thomas Regulator required repairs it was sent to the W.F. Plambeck Jewelry Company which was a watch inspector for the D & I as well as several other roads.—*CRRM*

Denver & Interurban Shop—This map of the new shop on Fox Street dates to the mid-1920s, shortly before abandonment and after the connection to the Denver Tramway's line had been removed.—*CRRM*

The M-157 waits in front of the shop shortly after the line opened and before the paving stones had been placed between the rails curving out to the street.—*Edmunds Collection*

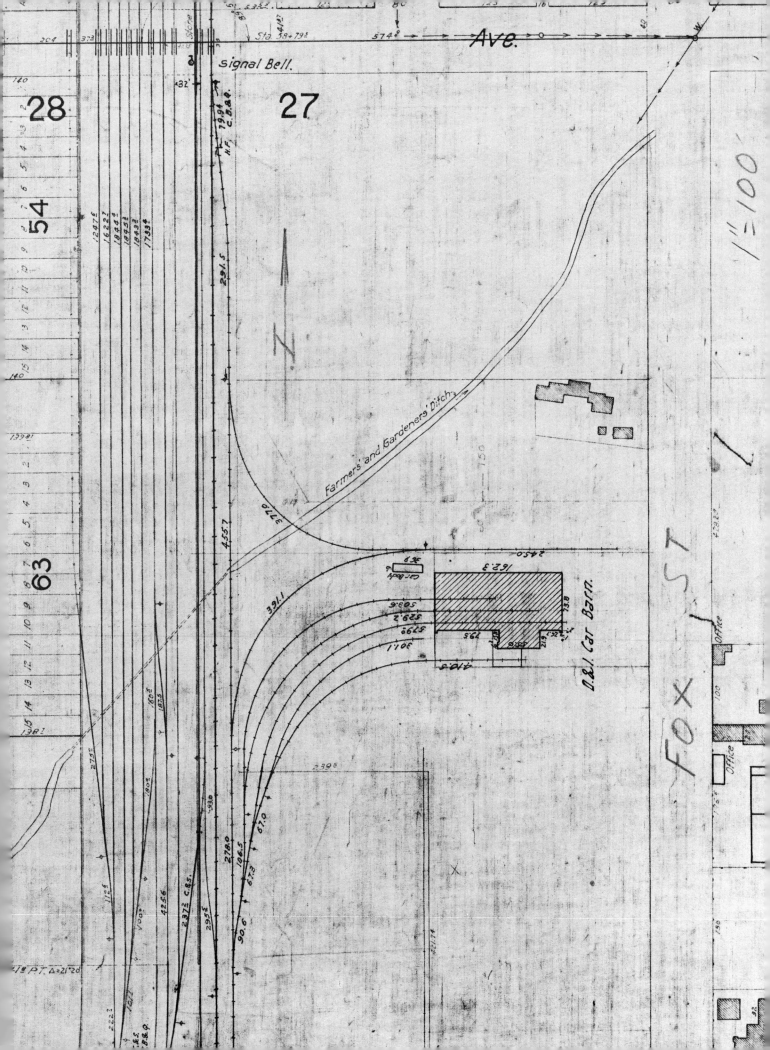

Ave.

signal Bell.

28   27

54

63

Farmers' and Gardeners' Ditch

N

O.B.I. Car Barn.

FOX ST.

Office

Office

1" = 100'

Several cars await assignments on the west side of the new shop at Thirty-sixth Avenue and Fox Street. The shop building is seen in May 1948 shortly before being razed for construction of the Valley Highway, later designated Interstate 25.—*Above, UCWH; Below, R. H. Kindig*

The interior of the new shop was photographed shortly after opening. Unlike the old shop, space did not permit car storage inside, but ample trackage was provided outside for that purpose.—*Both, CRRM*

These two photos taken from the wye alongside the new shop indicate the rural character of the location at this time. On the right the view is to the west across the Burlington track—now electrified for the D & I—then the C & S main line and the Denver & Salt Lake or Moffat Road. Below, the view is to the east with the track curving right onto Fox Street and a connection with the Tramway line over the Twenty-third Street viaduct. The poles for the Tramway's Globeville line can be followed along Fox Street but early in 1923 the D & I's connecting line was removed and all operations were via Union Station. The Tramway soon converted their line from standard gauge to forty-two-inch gauge to conform to all other city lines.—*Both, CRRM*

The Fort Collins Carbarn

The Fort Collins carbarn was located near the Colorado & Southern railroad yard, at the corner of Howes and Cherry streets. It was a large brick building with a substation in the rear. Electricity was purchased from Northern Colorado Power Company. A 500-kilowatt motor-generator set converted AC to DC. In 1919, the city of Fort Collins purchased this carbarn for use with its municipal railway. The city did not want the M-G set, so the D & I sold that to the power company.

By fall 1907 work was moving swiftly on the car barn and power house in Fort Collins as evidenced in these payment records.— CRRM

Dept. No. _____ Treas. No. _____ Audit No. **354**

The Denver & Interurban Railroad Company

Charge _____ To **Westinghouse Elec. Mfg. Co.** Dr.

_2/_ _354_ Of _____

Pay **Same.**

Month of _____ 190_ Address **Denver, Colo.**

For

First payment on account for Power House Machinery for Fort Collins Street Railway, as per terms of contract.

50% of $12,000.00.......................... $6000.00

ALLISON STOCKER, 2636 W. 27TH AVE. PHONE 3548 MAIN.
J. H. G. FRASER, 109 LOGAN AVE. PHONE 644 BROWN.

Denver, Colo., _11/1_ 190_7_

M _Denver & Interurban Ry_

Ft Collins

IN ACCOUNT WITH

460

STOCKER & FRASER,
GENERAL CONTRACTORS.

460

213 CONTINENTAL BLD'G.   TELEPHONE 882.

To contract for car barn	15023	00
" 6600 extra brick (change in plan)	66	00
	15089	00
Cr. by cash		14000 —
Balance	1089	00

The Interurban Power System

The electrical power system on the Denver & Interurban was unique. It was a single-phase, alternating current system at 11,000 volts and 25 hertz. For interurbans in 1908, this represented a radical new technology. Many in the industry felt that such a system would be doomed by unreliability and high maintenance costs. Although that assumption proved false, most lines chose tried and true direct current at 600 or 1,200 volts.

Electrical engineers from Westinghouse sold the D & I management on an AC system. Its advantages centered around efficiency in long distance power transmission and low construction costs. These were very important issues for a system having a proposed length of 110 miles. A 4/0 gauge wire will carry roughly fifteen times more current at 11,000 volts AC than it will at 550 volts DC. In addition, little energy is lost to wire resistance at the higher voltage.

The emergence of single-phase technology was important to railroads because single-phase AC requires only one trolley wire. Three-phase current is more commonly generated by utilities, but a three-phase railroad electrification requires two trolley wires.

The choice of 11,000 volts meant that no substations or feeder wires were needed on the D & I in order to deliver sufficient power to the interurban cars. All of the necessary power could be carried for the length of the system by the catenary. In addition, the catenary could be made of high strength bronze and steel, rather than copper, and still meet the needs of service. Bronze and steel have significantly less current carrying capacity than copper.

The 25 hertz power was required for traction motors. Large variable speed AC motors tend to run poorly on the 60 hertz power, which is American commercial frequency.

The drawbacks associated with AC were found on the cars that used it. These included transformers to produce a low voltage on the cars, heavy control equipment and complex traction motors. AC cars tended to weigh ten to fifteen percent more than DC cars of equal construction.

General Electric pushed the use of direct current. The car mounted equipment for DC was light and rugged but DC will not operate a transformer. This meant the voltage in the trolley wires could be no higher than that desired on board the cars. In order to effectively distribute current, DC lines typically required copper trolley wires, heavy copper feeder wires throughout the system and manned substations at intervals of five to twenty miles. All of these were expensive.

The Denver & Interurban's electrical distribution system was built by Westinghouse, Church, Kerr & Company, a contractor working for the

Northern Colorado Power Company's Lafayette plant under construction on February 24, 1907.—*Public Service Company of Colorado*

Northern Colorado Power Company. Included were a 2,000 kilowatt single-phase generating station in Lafayette, an 11,000 volt transmission line to D & I Junction, and forty-four miles of poles and catenary. Poles, bracket arms and catenary were installed by crews working from chartered Colorado & Southern steam trains. All work was carried out in accordance with D & I specifications and performed under the watchful eyes of D & I inspectors. The catenary was made of a 4/0, grooved, phono-electric trolley wire supported by a 7/16-inch galvanized steel cable messenger. Phono-electric is a bronze alloy. Galvanized iron hangers linked the messenger and trolley wires at ten-foot intervals. The catenary was suspended twenty-two feet above the rails and supported by approximately twenty-four hundred creosoted cedar poles. The rails were bonded and tied into a pole-mounted ground wire for current return.

The pole spacing ranged from 120 feet on straight track to 50 feet on ten degree curves. The trolley wire had a maximum divergence from track center of 3.5 inches. There was no staggering in the alignment of the trolley wires since the rocking of the cars was enough to prevent a groove from wearing into the pantograph head.

Within the city of Boulder, the overhead was a single copper trolley wire supported by steel poles. It was twenty feet above the street. Power for the 550-volt DC city line was supplied by a 300-kilowatt substation on Twelfth Street near the edge of town. The substation contained a motor-generator set for current conversion. An 11,000-volt AC motor which was fed from the catenary turned a 550-volt DC generator.

The D & I electrification was divided into twelve AC sections and one DC section. If overhead wire maintenance was required, the line crew could isolate those sections it was working on instead of being forced to work on the wires hot or to shut down the entire system for limited maintenance. Wire maintenance was a D & I responsibility even though the power company owned the wires.

Railroad electrification has a high cost, and this forty-four-mile project cost Northern Colorado Power Company a total of $188,000.00. The founders of the D&I convinced Northern Colorado Power to bear this burden after selling them on the benefits of having a large reliable customer within the sparsely settled lands they planned to serve. The D & I benefited through spreading its construction debts over more than one company, and by locking in some power rates which initially looked quite good. The power company paid for this construction work through the sale of bonds.

A contract between the two companies required the D & I to make 4.5 percent annual bond payments to the Central Trust Company of New York and five percent construction payments to Northern Colorado Power. The D & I was also required to pay $3,602.00 per month for keeping the generators on line and $.0025 per kilowatt for power used. Power usage was measured at the generating station in Lafayette. This allowed the power company to bill for any current which might be lost, or wasted on something other than car propulsion.

Bond payments equaling the total cost of construction were to be made over twenty years. At the conclusion of the payments, the D & I would own the electrification. The D & I was free to pay off the bonds early if it chose to, and construction payments were to cease whenever the bonds were paid. The construction payments essentially

In 1957, just fifty years after the construction photo at left, the plant had already been closed by Public Service and in a few years would be razed.—CRRM

represented interest paid to the power company.

According to the contract, the D & I could request sixty-six additional miles of single track electrification under these same terms. That was enough to reach Fort Collins and beyond.

The contract exempted the power company from liability for "acts of God, strike, riot, accidental fire, invasion, explosion, or public enemies either at the coal mines or the generating station." It also provided that if the power company failed to operate its plant for more than twelve hours after the railroad requested operation, then the railroad could take over the power plant and supply itself with power. Another clause stated that if the railroad's payments were overdue by sixty days or more, the power company was free to turn off the power and void the contract.

Electric power was very expensive on the Kite route. During bankruptcy hearings in 1919, the D & I pointed to its power rates as the biggest single source of financial problems. Although the contract rate was one-quarter of a cent per kilowatt, the D &

I was actually paying 2.42 cents per kilowatt if fixed charges were included in the calculation. William H. Edmunds, the line's receiver argued that a more reasonable rate would be one cent per kilowatt. The bankruptcy court judge considered this argument, but there was little which could be done to adjust the fixed charges. They paid for a power plant and catenary that served no other customers. The judge did, however, reduce the contract rate. He ruled that the kilowatt rate must be reduced from $.0025 to $.0015, saying "anything higher would be unreasonable." Western Power & Light accepted this rate reduction, since it was part of a plan to save a weak customer, but WP & L demanded that D & I reduce its power demand in exchange, allowing sale of power to other customers. The D & I agreed.

The rapidly growing Northern Colorado Power Company was renamed in 1915, becoming the Western Light & Power Company. The utility was purchased by the Public Service Company in 1923. The changes in name and ownership at the power company had no impact on the D & I contract.

Form 7-1M-10-14

The Western Light and Power Company

BOULDER, COLORADO November 30, 1914

355

Charges to   Denver & Interurban R. R. Co.
Denver, Colorado

355

355

Service Lafayette Nov. 1914

Reading	11/30	6204890					
"	10/31	5974190					
		230700 KWH at .0025		576	75		
		Fixed charge		3,602	00	4,178	75

4

APPROVED
W H Edmunds   4098
Elec. Engr. & Trainmaster.

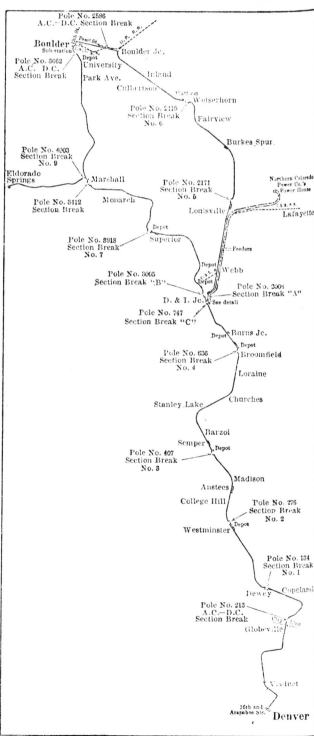

A substation was built on Twelfth Street in Boulder to provide 550-volt DC current for operation on the city streets. The building and its equipment are seen in these photos. The map at left indicates the locations of the various power sections on the 11,000-volt AC system. Western Light and Power Company, successor to Northern Colorado Power, billed the D & I monthly and charges such as that of $4,178.75 for November 1914, were one of the major fixed costs which caused the line to operate at a loss.—*Above and Below, Edmunds Collection; Others, CRRM*

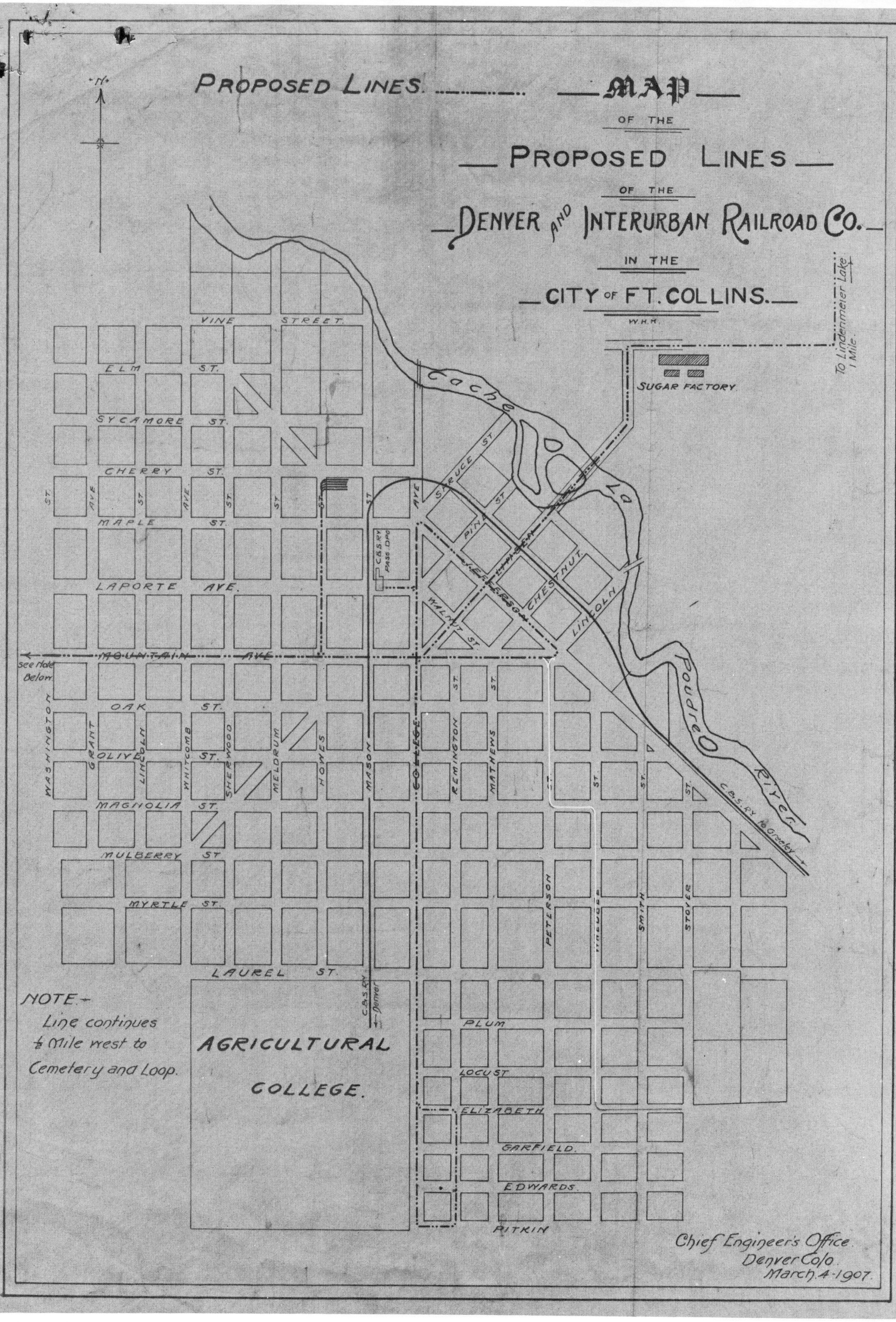

PROPOSED LINES. ———— ——— MAP —

OF THE

PROPOSED LINES

OF THE

Denver and Interurban Railroad Co.

IN THE

CITY of FT. COLLINS.

W.H.H.

-N-

To Lindenmeier Lake
1 Mile.

SUGAR FACTORY

Cache La Poudre River

VINE STREET

ELM ST.

SYCAMORE ST.

CHERRY ST.

MAPLE ST.

LAPORTE AVE.

C&S.RY
PASS. DPO

SPRUCE ST.
PINE ST.
LINDEN ST.
WILLOW ST.
CHESTNUT
WALNUT ST.
LINCOLN

MOUNTAIN AVE.

See Note
Below

OAK ST.

WASHINGTON
GRANT
OLIVE
LINCOLN
WHITCOMB
SHERWOOD
MELDRUM
HOWES
MASON
COLLEGE
REMINGTON
MATHEWS

ST.

MAGNOLIA ST.

MULBERRY ST.

MYRTLE ST.

PETERSON
SMITH
STOVER

C&S.RY to Greeley

C&S.RY
↑ Denver

LAUREL ST.

NOTE —
Line continues
½ Mile west to
Cemetery and Loop.

AGRICULTURAL

COLLEGE.

PLUM

LOCUST

ELIZABETH

GARFIELD.

EDWARDS

PITKIN

Chief Engineer's Office
Denver Colo.
March. 4. 1907.

4

Big Green Cars in the Streets

As was true with most interurban railroads, the Denver & Interurban line was routed through the streets of major towns. This provided direct access to downtown business districts, and to trackside residential areas. Convenience was a valuable selling point for D & I service before automobiles became commonplace. However, along with street operations came a host of varied and unexpected problems. The solution was to get off the streets. Between 1917 and 1922, the D & I did just that. How and why were a different story in each town.

The Fort Collins Street Railway

The Fort Collins Street Railway was planned as part of a hub for Denver & Interurban lines radiating out into the Northern Colorado countryside. Instead it became a small isolated branch of a mainline that never came to town.

On July 23, 1906, the city of Fort Collins granted right-of-way to the Denver & Interurban for the construction of its line, and a franchise for operation through town. In exchange, the D & I was to build at least five miles of line in town during 1907, and a minimum of a mile per year in 1908 and 1909. It would also have to offer streetcar service at twenty-minute intervals between 6:30 A.M. and 10:00 P.M. An annual franchise tax equaling three percent of the local service gross revenues would be due for the first ten years. This was to increase to four percent for the second ten years and five percent for the remaining term.

In 1907, the Denver & Interurban built 5.4 miles

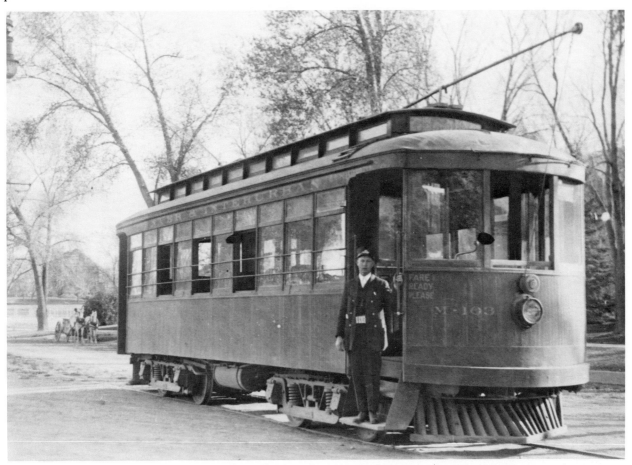

Fort Collins soon had an excellent streetcar system as seen in this classic photo of conductor and car posed ready to serve the public.— *CRRM*

of line extending onto Mountain Avenue, College Avenue, Jefferson Street, La Porte Street, Howe Street and Linden Street. Regular service began on January 1, 1908. There were no extensions within the city limits during 1908, but Fort Collins agreed to accept the 1.5 mile extension to reach the Lindenmeier Lake Resort as a substitute. During 1909, the D & I built a .95 mile extension along Whedbee Street and the city agreed to accept this as compliance with the terms of the franchise.

The D & I commitment to Fort Collins operations was a substantial one. At a time when station agents earned $1,830.00 per year and architects made $2,400.00, the D & I invested roughly $250,000.00 in order to build a first class system. There were six streetcars, two trailers, a carbarn and a 500-kilowatt substation all of which were built to equal any in the city of Denver. These were a source of pride for both the D & I and the citizens of Fort Collins.

Although Fort Collins was a small town, it had been growing at an impressive rate. Between 1900 and 1910, the population grew from 3,053 to 8,210. This was an increase of 168.9 percent. The Fort Collins Street Railway was over-built so that it could easily expand as the city expanded.

Unfortunately, Fort Collins stopped expanding. Its population grew by only 545 between 1910 and 1920. Instead of absorbing a few years of start-up losses as the line grew to prosperity, the D & I was faced with continuous and increasing losses. The lack of intercity connections, plus low population and low ridership within the city, left the streetcars under-utilized. The twenty-three-ton weight of cars resulted in high current consumption and the use of conductors as well as motormen resulted in high labor costs.

The D & I converted its Fort Collins cars to one man operations in 1914, but fares remained fixed at the city approved rate of five cents per ride. High inflation followed World War I and so did automobile ownership. The Fort Collins Street Railway was in serious trouble. In order to turn the situation around, the Denver and Interurban sought financial assistance from the city. Although a number of proposals were considered, there was no consensus in city hall that the city needed to help or should help. There was a valid franchise in force which required the D & I to operate the streetcars. In addition, it was well known that the D & I was owned by the profitable Colorado & Southern Railway. Many people felt that the C & S should simply pay the debts incurred by the D & I and forget about them. A court found for the C & S. According to the ruling, the C & S was a separate corporation, thus the D & I was liable for its own debts.

Action by the C & S in 1918 provided the D & I with the opportunity to permanently resolve the Fort Collins problems. The C & S owned all of the Denver & Interurban bonds, and no interest had been paid since 1914. Foreclosure papers were filed in Federal District Court on June 11, 1918, by the Guaranty Trust Company of New York. The trust company did this on behalf of bondholders, who chose not to focus attention upon themselves. Foreclosure forced the D & I into receivership. The court, acting upon advice from the bondholders, immediately appointed W. H. Edmunds, receiver. Edmunds was quite knowledgeable in how best to manage the D & I since he was its electrical engineer and trainmaster. On June 22, 1918, Edmunds presented the money losing history of the Fort Collins Street Railway to the court. He then asked for instructions regarding its future. The court, acting to protect the interests of the bondholders, ordered Edmunds to apply to the Public Utilities Commission for an emergency order to abandon operations. This order was granted on July 9, 1918, and operations ceased on July 10. The residents of Fort Collins were startled. The streetcar system which they viewed as a public necessity was suddenly gone.

Following abandonment, Edmunds negotiated to sell the line to the city. Several months without transit underscored a need for the city to act. On January 7, 1919, the voters overwhelmingly approved a municipal railway bond issue. The sale of tracks, carbarn and trolley wires was concluded on May 15, 1919.

Three of the big wooden streetcars were later sold to the Oklahoma Railway which ran them in Oklahoma City. The others were scrapped. The move from the streets of Fort Collins allowed the D & I to cut its losses and generated $53,000.00 which was applied toward the debts of the Denver-Boulder Kite Route.

The city owned Fort Collins Municipal Railway cut its losses by purchasing four lightweight, single truck Birneys to replace the seven big D & I green cars. The line continued to operate until June 30, 1951, when the streetcars were replaced by buses.

The M-102 was destroyed in a wreck with a steam shovel near the Great Western Sugar Company plant in 1915, miraculously with no loss of life. On a better day a car moves along Linden Street (left) soon after the line's opening. —Both, CRRM

In December 1984, thirty-three years after the trolleys stopped running in Fort Collins, the beautifully restored Birney car No. 21 again rolled down Mountain Avenue, the result of work by the Fort Collins Municipal Railway Society. Track construction continues and while a few dissidents opposed the project, the town has now taken the line to heart. On weekends when the car operates there lives a small reminder of the Denver & Interurban.—Al Kilminster

Boulder and the Kite Route

The first D & I car ran to Boulder on Tuesday, June 23, 1908. It was towed through the streets of Boulder by a steam engine, since the substation equipment was not yet installed and the 550-volt DC city overhead trolley line was dead.

Under an agreement with the city of Boulder, the D & I ran on Pearl Street, sixteen blocks to its depot in the rear of a bank at Twelfth. From there it went south on Twelfth Street two blocks to the Colorado & Southern line which ran through the University of Colorado campus. In return for the right to operate on the streets, the D & I had to carry local passengers and stop at any corner where Boulderites wanted to get on or off. It also had to pay for paving the 1.78 miles of streets it operated on and pay an annual franchise tax of 7.5 cents per capita, based on Boulder's population. When Western Light and Power Company got a franchise to serve the Boulder area, part of the agreement with Boulder stated that the power company would have to provide streetcar service in Boulder. Western Light and Power got together with the D & I and came to agreement about using the D & I tracks on Pearl Street as part of their route.

Within a few years after service started, the D & I became fully aware of the problems involved in running heavyweight interurban cars on the streets. Rail was wearing at a rapid rate. The railheads were being ground off at the tight radius curves and switches, while broken rail was a common problem on straight sections. Frequent replacement of rail was a real headache. The D & I had to dig up the street to replace the rail, and then pay the city to have the street repaved. Soon after these problems arose, the D & I began mulling over ways to get off the streets and instead use C & S steam trackage through town. The problem was getting the Boulder City Council and the Public Utilities Commission to approve such a move. Many Boulderites were against it because they liked having the big green cars conveniently providing rides down Pearl Street. Also, they liked the D & I's nice little business district depot. One petition protested the move on the grounds that the C & S depot was "so dark, dismal, and dirty, that women and children dare not use it."

As approval for the change seemed nearer, the D & I deferred maintaining the track and by May 1917, things were coming to a head. The city was preparing to repave Pearl Street and bill the D & I

By the clock on the First National Bank building it is just five minutes until departure and the crowd is anxious to board the two-car D & I train at the Boulder depot on this morning in 1916. At 9:30 A.M. the train will head south on Twelfth Street, join the C & S line to Marshall and be in Denver at 10:40 A.M.—*Both, E. J. Haley Collection*

Boulder—Pearl Street

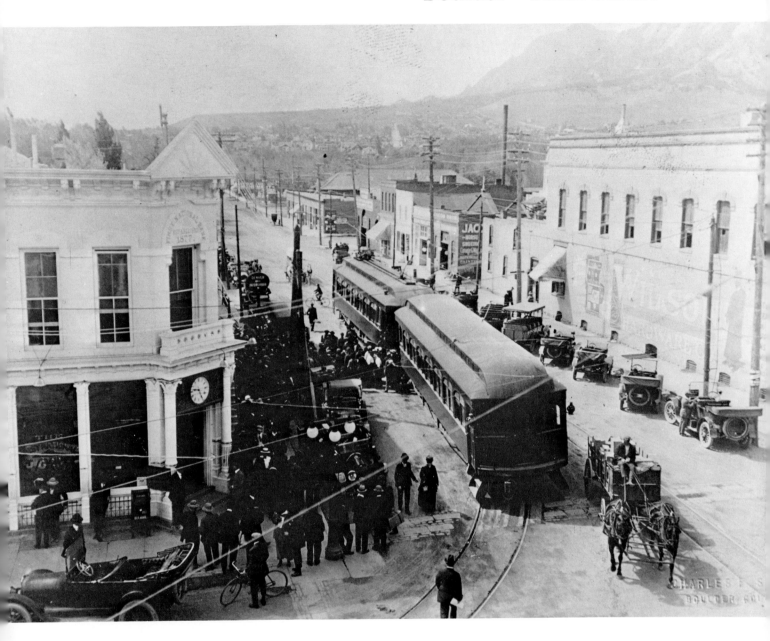

for it. The Boulder station agent complained that the rail was broken in thirty different places and causing current return problems. Whenever the cars ran, there were flaming rail joints and it was impossible for a three-car train to make it through town.

The D & I was anxious to get off the streets as soon as possible and argued in hearings that its cars were too large to be used in street railway service. It also agreed to pay half of the $8,000 paving assessment for 1917 even if its cars were not using the street. To make certain the Western Power did not oppose the move, the D & I offered to donate the street trackage poles and overhead to the power company's streetcar line.

The Boulder City Council approved the move on June 23, 1917, and the PUC approved shortly thereafter. The D & I cars immediately began service to the C & S depot with the help of steam engines. An 11,000-volt catenary was soon hung along the C & S line and the D & I's burdensome street trackage problems were over. Western Power accepted the donated street route, and the D & I sold the unneeded 550-volt motor-generator to the Denver Tramway.

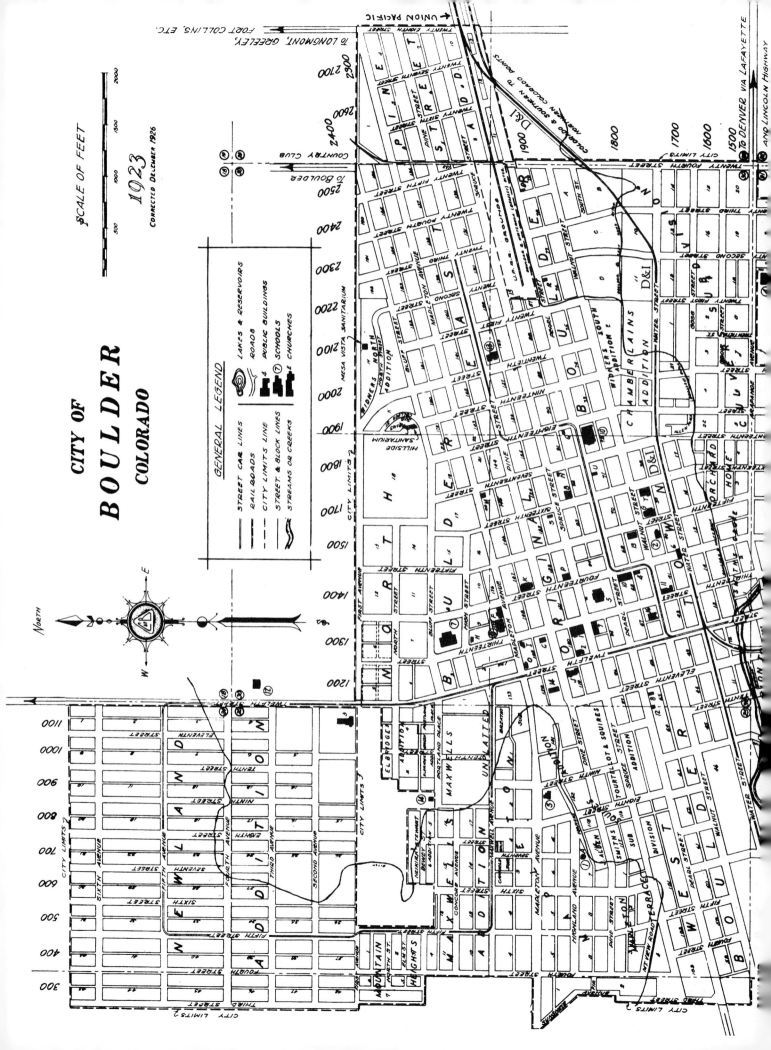

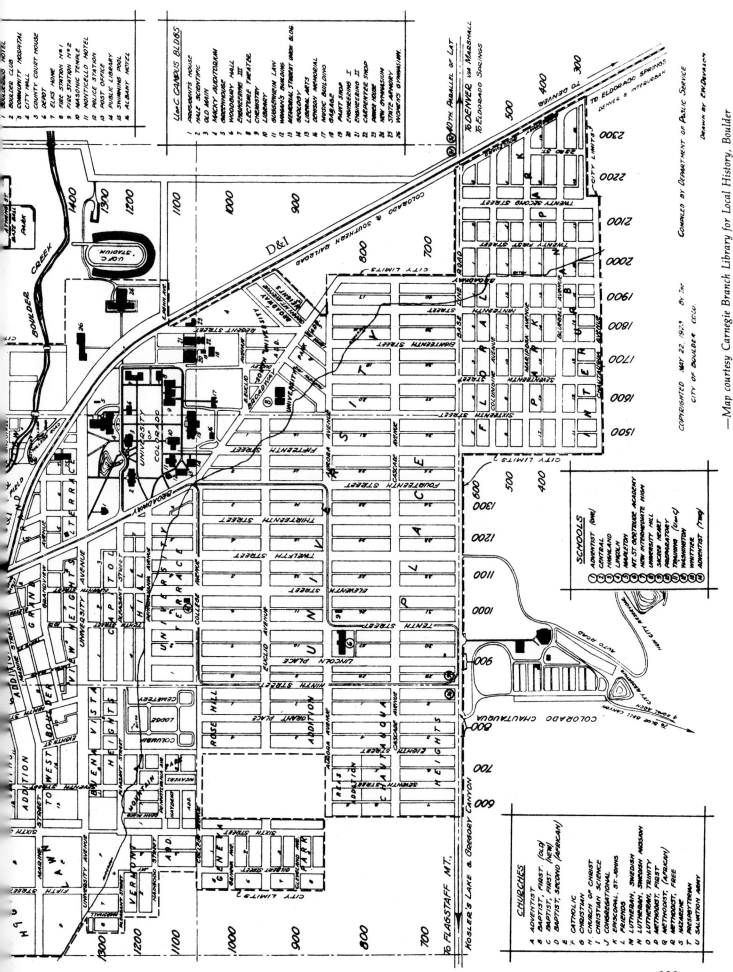

—Map courtesy Carnegie Branch Library for Local History, Boulder

101

This was the engineer's view from an interurban as it crossed Arapahoe Street with the bridge over Boulder Creek approaching and downtown Boulder just beyond. From the bridge a car is seen approaching from the south.— *Both, CRRM*

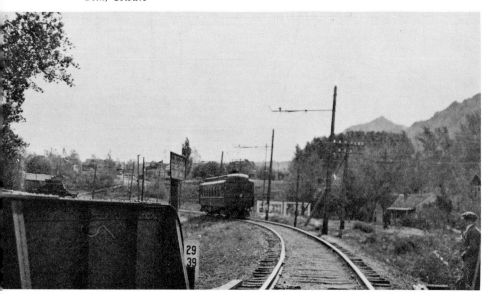

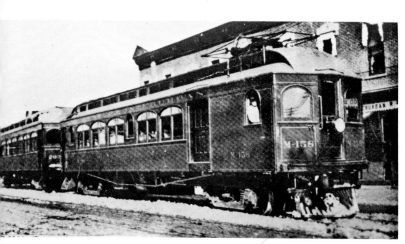

The M-158 and a trailer wait at the D & I station in the back of the First National Bank building on Twelfth Street just around the corner from Pearl Street in this 1913 scene reproduced from a post card.—*CRRM*

It is difficult in the mid-1980s to locate traces of the D & I/C & S line across the University of Colorado campus. This photo and the accompanying map illustrate the route the line followed past the power house—still standing—the small station just beyond and then curved northwest to cross Broadway and then curve back east to the C & S station. In earlier years the D & I left the C & S at Twelfth Street to run along Pearl Street and rejoin the C & S east of Boulder. Broadway can be seen along the lower left of the photo and then curves northward to intersect the railroad.– *Above, UCWH*

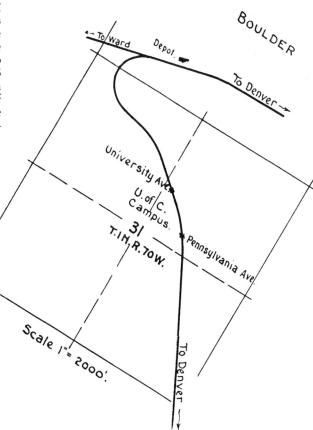

BOULDER

To Ward

Depot.

To Denver

University Ave.

U. of C. Campus.

Pennsylvania Ave.

31
T. 1 N., R. 70 W.

Scale 1" = 2000'.

To Denver

ARA

ARA, a location previously known as Boulder Junction was where the C & S and Union Pacific crossed and interchanged and also the point at which the D & I left the C & S mainline to begin running along Pearl Street. Today the Burlington Northern crosses Pearl at this same location, but the Union Pacific has been abandoned back two miles to Valmont. Below, a two car train has paused on Pearl Street while in the lower view a five car train has stopped on Pearl near Thirtieth Street, the point at which the changeover was made from AC to DC for city running with the trolley poles. —*Below, Edmunds Collection; Bottom, R.H. Kindig Collection; Map, Colorado Public Utilities Commission*

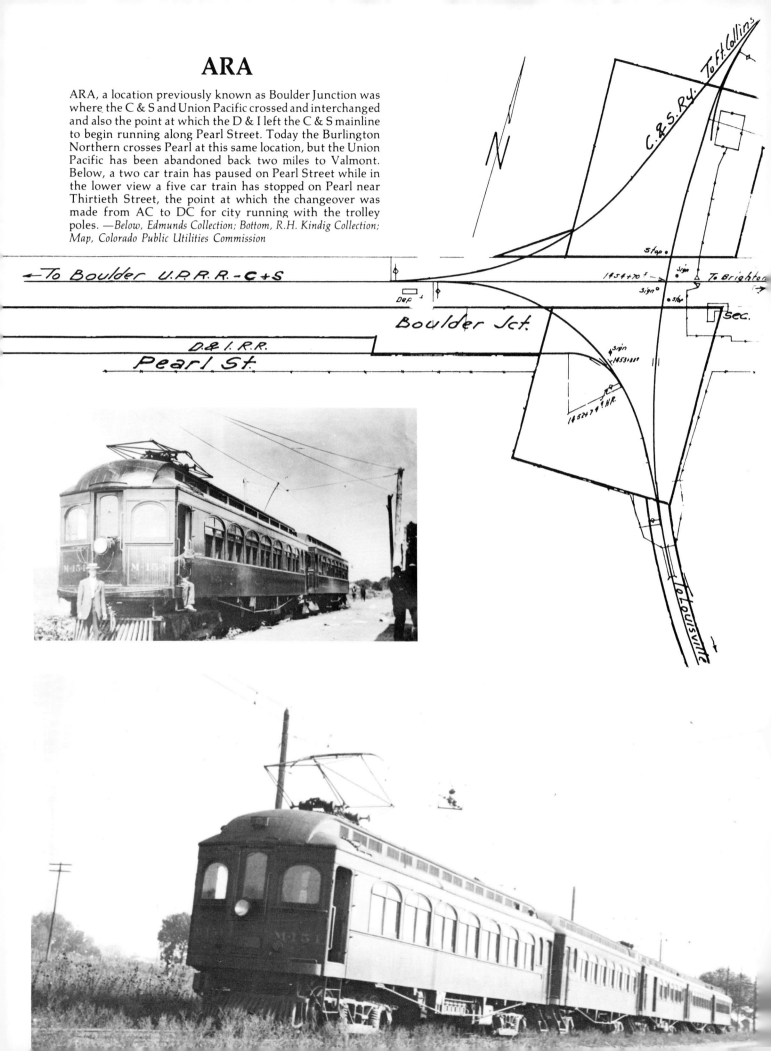

Boulder—C & S Station

A five car train waits in the Boulder station after the D & I had ended all street running in Boulder. Below, on October 24, 1924 a big green interurban approaches the Twenty-fourth Street crossing eastbound enroute to Denver. Today this once rural location is in the heart of Boulder near the intersection of Twenty-fourth and South streets.—*Above, Edmunds Collection; Below, CRRM*

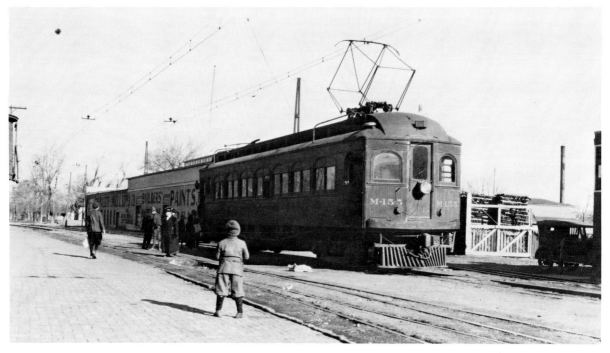

The M-155 looms huge to a youngster on the brick platform of the Boulder station circa 1920. When the D & I reached agreement with the city of Boulder to stop operating on Pearl Street, they immediately moved to the C & S station and while awaiting installation of overhead electrification used a steam engine for power as billed below to the D & I by the C & S.—*Both, CRRM*

Form 2850-1st Rev.-4-17-15M.

BILL COLLECTIBLE

WHEN REMITTING
PLEASE QUOTE

DEPARTMENT NO. D-3508

AUDIT NO.

DATE April 13th, 1918

RECORDED IN Mar. 1918

Denver & Interurban Railroad Company,

ADDRESS Denver, Colorado

To The Colorado & Southern Railway Co., Dr.

REMITTANCES SHOULD BE MADE TO B. F. JAMES, TREASURER, DENVER, COLO.

FOR use of facilities at Boulder, Colo. during the month of September, 1917:			APPROVED
Handling trains btw. Boulder Jct. and University:			
Hire of Eng. 101 - 1st. to 20th incl.	20 days		SUPERINTENDENT
" 213 - 21st to 27th "	7 "		
	27 "	@$15.00	$405.00
Fuel - 216 tons @ 2.00	432.00		
Frt. - " " 2.50 T	540.00		
Water - 54 Tanks .50 tank	27.00		
Supplies - 27 days .30	8.10		
Lubricants - 27 " .30	8.10		
Enginehouse Exp. 27 days @ $3.00	81.00		1096.20
Wages-Enginemen			487.05
Passenger Station Facilities			100.00
			$2088.25

DO NOT ALTER BILL. IF EXCEPTION IS TAKEN, RETURN TO J. H. BRADBURY, GENERAL AUDITOR, DENVER. COLO., FOR CORRECTION, STATING OBJECTIONS.

AUDITED:

APPROVED FOR COLLECTION

ASSISTANT GENERAL AUDITOR.

The Route into Denver

The cars of the Denver & Interurban Railway reached Interurban Loop in downtown Denver by running for 4.13 miles on a standard gauge line of the Denver Tramway. The D & I was under no particular pressure to cease running its cars on Denver's streets. The tracks were owned and maintained by the Denver Tramway Company and since there was a flat rate contract, the D & I did not significantly share in the unexpected economic burdens that arose from its street operations.

In 1906, when the D & I was in the planning stage, D & I officials met with those of the Denver Tramway Company to work out an agreement for entrance into the city. The Tramway already had an exclusive franchise for street railway service and already occupied most of the streets that the D & I would need to use. The two groups arrived at an agreement that seemed fair to both sides, and a twenty-year contract was signed on April 17, 1906. Its stated purpose was to provide for an interchange of traffic for better public accommodations.

According to this contract, there would be an interchange at Fifty-second and Washington streets in Globeville. At this point, the D & I cars would leave the private right-of-way and be turned over to Tramway crews for operation on a proposed new city line. Since most of the Tramway cars were built to forty-two-inch gauge, three-rail track would be laid from Globeville to Interurban Loop so as to handle the cars of both companies. The Tramway agreed to pick up and discharge passengers along its route, and all passengers would pay Tramway a five cent fare for their trip through town. Though the D & I had to pay for laying the third rail, the Tramway agreed to do all track maintenance and to strengthen the Twenty-third Street viaduct so that it could handle D & I cars. After signing the contract, the Tramway decided against building a dual gauge line. Instead it built a two-rail, standard gauge line to Globeville and converted some of its cars to standard gauge in order to provide local service. The D & I was still assessed a fee as per the contract.

For its part, the Denver & Interurban agreed to "purchase and maintain suitable cars adapted for

Jessie J. Andis in the cab and John Bindley, conductor pose proudly with Denver & Interurban M-155 between runs in downtown Denver on Thirteenth Street between Arapahoe and Curtis streets in 1912. The Denver Tramway building is visible at extreme left.—*R.H. Kindig Collection*

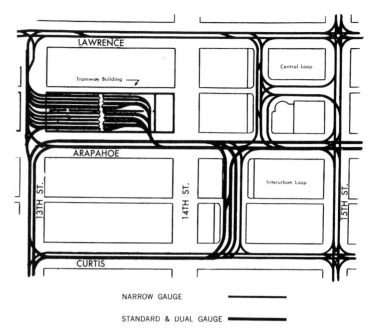

THE LOOPS & TRAMWAY BUILDING
1911

NARROW GAUGE ————————

STANDARD & DUAL GAUGE ▬▬▬▬▬▬▬

In 1910 the D & I began to operate from the Denver Tramway's Interurban Loop. The nearby Central Loop handled most city streetcar lines and thus D & I passengers could easily transfer to a car going almost anywhere on the Tramway system. The Central Loop is seen at left and at upper left Tramway Conductor Sam Wheeler and Motorman Fred Neff pose behind trailer 204 in the Interurban Loop prior to a run on the city line to Globeville where D & I crews took over operations. The Loop is seen in the bottom view about 1910 and at right shortly before the move to Union Station in September 1922.—*Map and Right, Intermountain Chapter, NRHS; Below, Edmunds Collection; Lower Left, Noel Holley Collection; Others, CRRM*

use and operation on the city line." It also agreed to do no local business within the city limits.

The first of the problems between the two companies arose after the Tramway rebuilt the Twenty-third Street viaduct. Previous to the construction of the D & I cars, the Tramway people were verbally told that the weight of the cars would not exceed fifty tons including load. When the cars entered service, they were found to weigh sixty-eight tons including load. The viaduct was being strained dangerously and in December 1908, the Tramway asked for additional payments to cover a major reconstruction job. The D & I refused to pay, and since the contract did not call for it to pay for rebuilding or maintenance costs, there was little the Tramway could do. The Tramway made some makeshift modifications to the viaduct to increase its capacity and allowed the cars to continue running. There were other problems too. The Tramway complained that the D & I cars were wearing out track and switches at an excessive rate and consuming enormous amounts of current. Having little recourse in these problems, the Tramway called for contract arbitration and, in the meantime, re-wound the motors on all D & I cars so as to reduce their current demand.

In 1911, the arbitrators awarded the Tramway an additional six cents per car mile to cover excess car weight. That fee was to be paid on top of the flat rate payments the D & I was making for interchange operations. In addition, the D & I contributed $3,000.00 in labor and materials toward strengthening the viaduct. This helped to ease the Tramway's problems and restore a feeling of fairness to the contract, but the viaduct was still weak. It should have been replaced with a much heavier steel structure, but no one offered to cover the expense of such a project. As a result, the city of Denver placed restrictions on the use of the Twenty-third Street viaduct. No more than one motorized D & I car was to cross it at a time. In addition, the speed was not to exceed eight miles per hour on the portion supported by wooden trestles and two miles per hour on the steel truss section.

The Denver and Interurban's other problems with the Tramway were few. The only complaint that the D & I had was about the Tramway crews. Most Tramway men were unfamiliar with how to operate the dual voltage Westinghouse controls on D & I cars and were causing a lot of delays. Regardless, the Tramway refused to permit D & I men to run the cars within the city limits. This problem was never really resolved until the D & I left the streets.

It wasn't until 1917 that the D & I began giving serious consideration to making Union Station its Denver terminal. In July of that year, the city of Denver condemned the Twenty-third Street viaduct as unsafe and ordered it rebuilt at the expense of the Tramway and/or the D & I. The city then sent in its own crews to give the structure a proper rebuilding. It was the D & I cars that were overloading the viaduct, but the city's franchise with the Denver Tramway made that company responsible for the rebuilding and maintenance. During the ninety days that the viaduct was closed, the D & I cars were pulled into Union Station by C & S steam power, and maintenance was performed at the C & S coach yard. The cars were picked up and delivered north of town at Modern Junction. Though this service was costing the D & I $3,000.00 per month, that was still $800.00 per month less than the cost of using the Tramway route. What is more, the D & I was now charging a five-cent city fare just as the Tramway had, but the money went into D & I coffers. Since the line was operating in the red, any idea that would save money and produce more revenue looked great. The D & I announced to the public that it was considering a permanent switch.

In Denver, the loudest response came from the Tramway. That company disliked the idea primarily because it did not want to lose the fares it was getting from D & I passengers. In a letter to the D & I management, the Tramway suggested that the best way for the D & I to save money was to stop all of its cars at Globeville. All passengers should be transferred to Tramway streetcars and the D & I would not have to pay for operating its cars on the city line. The Denver & Interurban felt that this suggestion was unacceptable.

Denver residents didn't say much at the time about the proposal to get the green cars off the street, but in 1910 there had been a lot of complaints about the cars. In that year, the Board of Public Works acting on complaints from Denver residents, branded the cars "a constant menace to life and traffic."

Boulderites weren't too concerned about safety in the Denver streets or schemes to save the D & I money. They objected to the move because Union Station was less convenient as a Denver terminal than Interurban Loop. Instead of walking across the street to take their choice of streetcar lines at Central Loop, they had to walk or ride six long blocks to reach it. Also many Boulderites were irate about having to pay a five-cent city fare to the D & I. Since it was not a Tramway fare, it did not cover free transfers to the Tramway's city lines. The Tramway had a right to charge for travel on its city lines, but the D & I had no legal basis for charging extra fares if the cars went to Union Station. The D & I tried to call it a Colorado & Southern fee, but

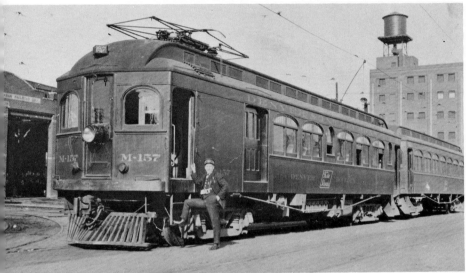

One of the few photos of a D & I car running downtown is this view of M-157 on Twenty-third Street passing the shop at Market Street. It appears a crew member has run from the shop and jumped aboard the engineer's compartment as the photo was taken. The same car, this time with a trailer is seen another day posed in front of the shop.— *Both, CRRM*

even the passengers knew the money was not going to the C & S.

When work on the viaduct was completed, the big green cars went back to the streets, but plans were in the works for a change. Not only was using Union Station cheaper, it would allow D & I motormen to operate all of the way into Denver. This would eliminate delays and prevent Tramway strikes from affecting D & I service. Many company memos bore the heading "Eliminate Tramway handling to reduce expenses and increase revenues." These were important considerations since the company was in receivership at the time.

Though the idea of making Union Station the permanent D & I terminal in Denver sounded good to the company management, no immediate change could be made. The big green heavyweights continued to wind their way through Denver streets for five more years while additional difficulties were ironed out.

The most important problems were all tied to the location of the carbarn and shop building. The barn was located at Twenty-third and Market streets, a location near the east end of the Twenty-third Street viaduct. To reach the barn, it was necessary to run on the tracks of the Denver Tramway Company and, of course, that meant retaining DC equipment in the cars. If Union Station was to be the terminal, the cars needed to be double ended. Only in this way could the time consuming process of wyeing and backing into the station be avoided. The work to install rear-end controls could not be carried out, though, until the DC equipment was removed.

It was quite apparent that new shop facilities would be needed in order to make a change of

AUTHORITY FOR EXPENDITURE.

THE DENVER AND INTERURBAN RAILROAD COMPANY.

~~The Colorado & Southern Railway Co.~~

Vice-President's No. 985   B & B   Dept.   March 27, 1911.   191

Authority is asked for the expenditure of $ 2929.27

for   Strenghtening 23rd Street Viaduct by reinforcing chord and putting in new frame bents between all old bents.

as per the following estimates:

26	12x12-28'	8736'			
36	12x12-26'	11232'			
41	12x12-24'	11808'			
39	12x12-22'	10298'			
34	12x12-20'	8160'			
9	12x12-18'	1944'			
5	12x12-16'	960'	53136'		
10	10x20-20'	3333'			
10	10x16-208	2664'	6000'		
68	3x10-24'	4080'			
75	3x10-20'	3750'			
38	3x10-18'	1710'			
20	3x10-16'	800'			
84	3x10-14'	2940'			
52	3x10-12'	1560'	14840'		
2	2x4-18'	24'			
8	1x6-16'	64'	88'		
200	Lbs Boat Spikes,			5.00	
200	Lbs O G Washers,			10.00	
110	3/4x20 Machine Bolts,			11.31	
585	3/4x18 Machine Bolts,			55.46	
240	3/4x16 Drift Bolts,			16.80	
200	Lbs Nails,			6.00	
1480	Lbs Cast Washers,			36.26	
647	Lin Ft 8x16 Old,	6897'	10.00	68.97	
173	Lin Ft 12x12 Old,	2076'	10.00	20.76	
6	Lin Ft 12x14 Old,	84'	10.00	.84	
72	Pcs 7x8-9' Old,	3024'	10.00	30.24	
				2256.57	
	Labor,			640.70	
	Teaming,			32.00	$2929.27

Reasons why the above expenditure is recommended

To make 23rd street viaduct safe for D&I motor cars.

Charge   *Maintenance*   *J H Bradbury*

Addition and betterments, $

Repairs (extraordinary), $

Replacements

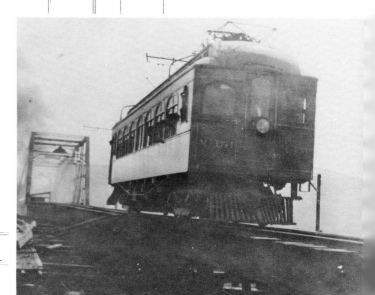

Correct: *E F Vines*   Recommended: *J Welsh*

ASST CHIEF ENGINEER.   GENERAL SUPERINTENDENT.

The D & I agreed to spend almost $3,000.00 to assist the Tramway in strengthening the Twenty-third Street viaduct and to also pay an additional fee due to the high cost of operating the heavy interurbans on the city line. The viaduct is seen opposite and an interurban appears in the lower view crossing at very restricted speed. D & I cars followed the Tramway's Globeville route visible in these two views believed taken on Washington Street. The car in the lower photo is Denver & Intermountain No. 21, usually assigned to Denver-Golden service. Globeville service was normally handled by cars 240, 241, and 248 which had been converted from forty-two-inch gauge to standard gauge for this purpose.—*Photos Opposite, Edmunds Collection; Right, Kenton Forrest Collection; Others, CRRM*

Denver, Colo., **Jan. 7** , **1915.**   **408**

The Denver & Interurban Railroad Co.,
   Denver, Colo.

408

Registered in

.........**December** ...... **1914**....... }

       To THE DENVER TRAMWAY COMPANY, Dr.

This Bill must be made in copying ink and sent to the Auditor for Copying.

For increased cost of handling your cars between Globeville and the Loop in accordance
   with finding of Mr. H. S. Crocker, dated
   Dec. 19, 1911, of 6¢ per car mile as follows:

Date	Motor Mileage
December-1914	4,468.47

Less: Deadhead motor mileage
     included in this company's
     Audit No. 3055 --------------   153.27
          Total Miles--------   4,315.20

4,315.20 car miles @ 6¢ per car mile = $258.91

Globeville

The Denver Union Terminal Ry. Co.
SUPPLEMENT No. 1
TO
UNION STATION TIME TABLE No. 31

Effective September 12, 1917, and until further notice, Denver & Interurban trains (formerly operated from and to Interurban Loop, 14th and Arapahoe Sts.), will be operated by the Colorado & Southern Railway, from and to Denver Union Station, on the following schedule, between Denver and Boulder:

DEPART				ARRIVE			
No.	Time	No.	Time	No.	Time	No.	Time
303	6:20 am	319	3:00 pm	302	7:45 am	318	4:50 pm
305	8:00 am	321	4:00 pm	304	8:50 am	320	5:50 pm
307	9:00 am	323	5:00 pm	306	10:50 am	322	6:50 pm
309	10:00 am	325	6:00 pm	308	11:50 am	324	7:50 pm
311	11:00 am	327	7:00 pm	310	12:50 pm	326	8:50 pm
313	12:00 n	329	8:00 pm	312	1:50 pm	328	9:50 pm
315	1:00 pm	331	9:00 pm	314	2:50 pm	330	10:50 pm
317	2:00 pm	333	11:25 pm	316	3:50 pm	332	11:59 pm

J. KEATING, Manager.

The Globeville station was in a small rented building at 5125 Washington Street. In 1913 owner John Bohte charged $25.00 monthly. No photo of the station is known to exist, but the building is now used as a home and is shown at upper right in 1986. Below is a rare view of crews changing in front of the Globeville station. Washington Street is unpaved in this view from Fifty-third Avenue looking south. The station is beyond the overpass which had been built to carry slag trains over the street from the Globe smelter on the west side. While the Twenty-third Street viaduct underwent repairs in fall 1917, a C & S steam engine was used to bring D & I cars directly into Union Station as noted in this special Denver Union Terminal timetable. This brief detour caused the D & I to give serious consideration to a permanent move from the city streets.—*Upper Right, William Jones; Others, CRRM*

terminals, but due to the company's financial position, there was no rush to put up a new building. Any new investment needed a lot of study since the line might not make it out of receivership. Not only were D & I officials concerned about making the right decision, officials of the Burlington and the Colorado & Southern were also looking closely at how their financially troubled subsidiary spent money.

The idea of doing repair work at the C & S coach yard was investigated. This, however, proved unacceptable since there were no pits, no sheds and no power for electrical tests. Having the work done in the shops of the C & S or the Burlington was investigated, but the idea proved too expensive. High wages in the steam shops, plus hostling charges would double the maintenance bill.

In 1920, the D & I management settled on the idea of putting up a new building at Thirty-sixth and Fox streets in a growing industrial district. By 1921, approval was received from the Burlington and the C & S. The new building cost $55,000.00 and was built in such a way that it could be sold as factory space if the line folded. The old barn, which was large enough to store twelve cars indoors, was to be sold for $60,000.00 to cover the cost of the new one. The new building was a complete shop, but it did not provide for car storage.

Several new routes were considered for entry into Denver. Proposal Number One involved electrifying some little used Burlington Railroad tracks from Utah Junction to a point beside the new shops at Thirty-sixth and Fox. There the D & I cars would enter the street and follow the Tramway line into Interurban Loop. Proposal Number Two was to electrify the Colorado & Southern line from Modern Junction and enter either Union Station or a small depot in the C & S coach yard, beneath the Sixteenth Street viaduct.

Proposal Number One had the drawback of requiring continued use of the Twenty-third Street viaduct. However, it was hoped that the Tramway fees might be significantly reduced because of lower car mileage on the Tramway line. Unfortunately the Tramway was in receivership at the time the proposal was made. The receivers provided no response.

Proposal Number Two had drawbacks also. The C & S line entering Denver was very busy and there was a distinct possibility that C & S traffic might interfere with D & I schedules. In addition, a terminal under the Sixteenth Street viaduct would be inconvenient to customers, and at Union Station the line might have to pay a hefty terminal fee. All railroads entering Union Station were members of the Denver Union Terminal Railway partnership and paid a share of the station's operating expenses.

The D & I escaped this fee in 1917 because of Colorado & Southern assistance. In response to complaints from the station's other tenants, the C & S argued that no fee was due because Denver & Interurban cars were only extra C & S passenger trains, if they were pulled by C & S steam engines. The proposed operation of D & I cars under their own power was another matter. The D & I would be liable for a fee equal to those paid by such railroads as the Union Pacific, the Rio Grande, the Rock Island, the Santa Fe, the Burlington and the Colorado & Southern. In addition, the terminal agreement gave these railroads veto power over the entrance of any railroad powered by an overhead trolley, or third rail.

A third proposal for entering Denver was the one which was adopted. Burlington tracks were electrified as far as a point adjacent to Union Station, but lying on C & S coach yard property. There a platform was built. The D & I terminated at the eleventh and twelfth tracks out from the depot building. Passengers reached the platform through an underground walkway that connected with the one owned by Union Station. The terminal company partners grudgingly agreed to this arrangement as a result of pressure by the Colorado & Southern. In exchange for a fee of $565.00 per month, the terminal company agreed to officially consider the cars and employees of the D & I to be cars and employees of the C & S.

The route into Union Station was ready to use by mid-summer, 1922, but the D & I did not change terminals until fall, because the interurban cars were not double-ended. They had to be wyed at the shop and backed one mile to the depot. To avoid this delay, the D & I handled its heavy summer traffic out of Interurban Loop. Following its change of terminals on Sunday, September 24, the D & I began negotiating to buy its way out of the twenty-year contract with the Tramway. While negotiations dragged, the D & I made occasional use of the Tramway route from Thirty-seventh and Fox to Interurban Loop. As a result, the city of Denver pressured both of them. The city was beginning a paving project and wanted the Tramway to immediately remove any rails which would no longer be used.

It also wanted the big green heavyweights off of the Twenty-third Street viaduct. On October 10, 1922, the city gave the D & I ten days to cease use of the viaduct. That order was ignored and the D & I continued to use the streets until December 22, 1922. After that date, the D & I ceased to be a street railway in any sense of the word, though it operated into Union Station until abandonment of service in 1926.

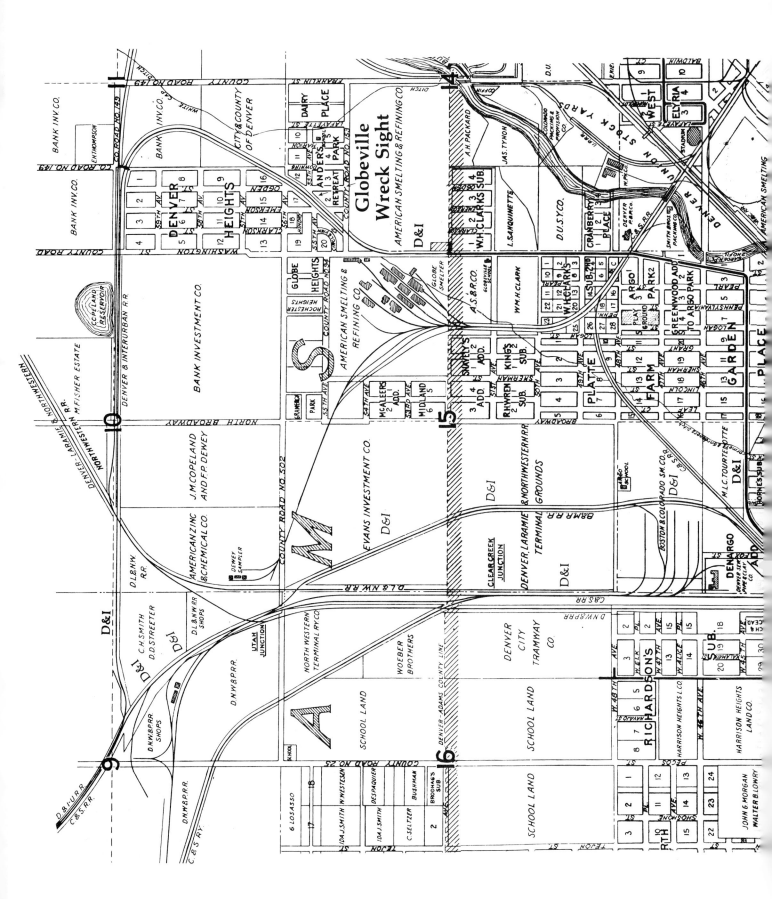

Globeville Wreck Sight

AMERICAN SMELTING & REFINING CO.

116

The D & I Routes in Denver

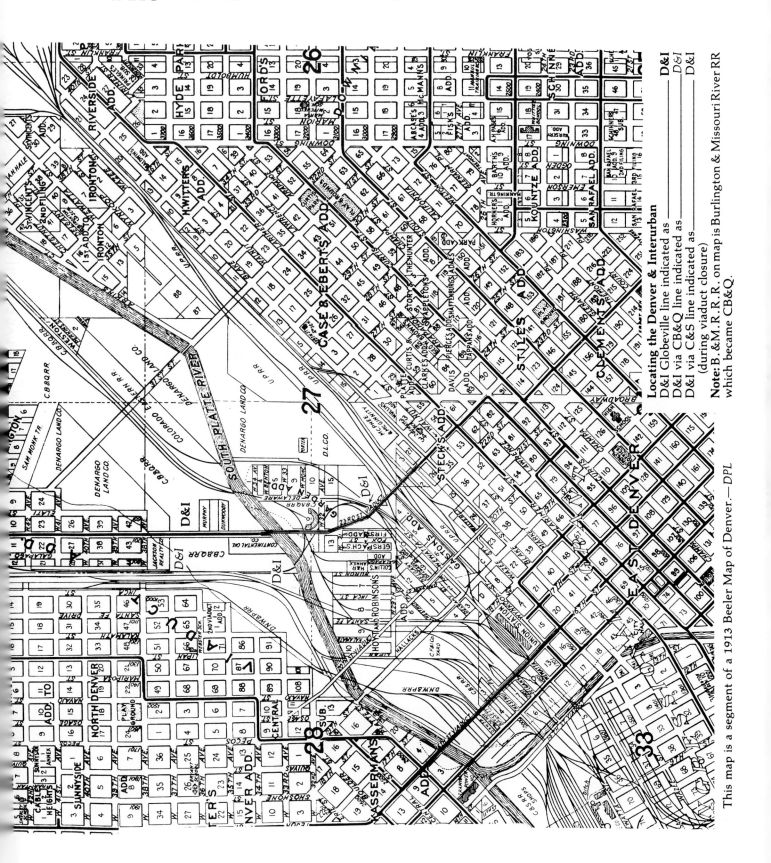

This map is a segment of a 1913 Beeler Map of Denver.—DPL

117

The Denver Union Terminal Ry. Co.

SAFETY
·D·U·T·
FIRST

TIME TABLE

No. 55

EFFECTIVE SEPTEMBER 24, 1922.

MOUNTAIN TIME

Effective Sept. 24, 1922, Denver & Interurban trains (formerly operated from and to Interurban Loop, 14th and Arapahoe Sts.) will be operated from and to Denver Union Station.

This is Denver Union Station as it appeared
to Denver & Interurban passengers. The
$565.00 monthly charge as shown on the
March 1923 bill was still a major savings over
operating costs on the city streets.—*Photo,
Noel Holley Collection; Bill, CRRM*

I. C. C. PERMANENTLY   FORM A-21---9-21-5M

Bill No. 8533

Denver and Interurban Railroad Company   Denver, Colo., **March 1, 1923**

Registered in
March, 1923

To THE DENVER UNION TERMINAL RAILWAY COMPANY, Dr.

Make checks payable to The Denver Union Term. Ry. Co. and address all remittances to Room 3, Denver Union Station.

For   use of Facilities of The Denver Union
       Terminal Railway Company for the month
       of MARCH,1923,per contract dated Mar.1,1922 $565.17

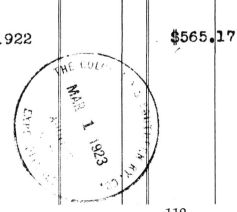

Moments before sunset a two-car train
accelerates after clearing Denver Union
Station on Sunday, October 1, 1922, just
seven days after the start of service from the
station as noted in the timetable.—*Otto Perry
Photo, E.J. Haley Collection; Timetable, CRRM*

A two-car train headed by M-157 passes the new shop (out of view to the right) just minutes from the end of its run at Union Station.—*CRRM*

Stacks of the Argo smelter and the Denver Sewer Pipe and Clay Company fill the horizon in this view of the D & I's Forty-eighth Avenue crossing on August 8, 1923. From the same crossing a southbound car approaches at right and below, this interesting photo was taken from about Fifty-first Avenue with the newly constructed Burlington-C & S shop on the right and the track curving northwest toward Utah Junction.—*All, CRRM*

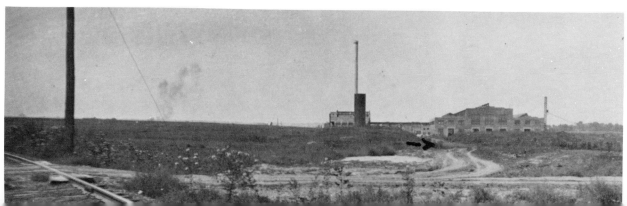

The Burlington's line north from Union Station had only light traffic and thus was ideal to be electrified as the D & I route out of Denver. At the time this was a rural area as seen in this pair of photos taken by the D & I following a collision with an automobile in July 1°22. The view above is from about Forty-ninth Avenue with a track curving south and slightly east, across the Forty-eighth Avenue crossing where the car is posed, then in the distance gently curving to the southwest for the run into Union Station. The city can be seen faintly in the distance. Below, the photographer faced in exactly the opposite direction. The track crosses Forty-eighth Avenue heading north and slightly west and then curves gently to head due north.—*Both, CRRM*

The big interurbans were capable of handling considerable snow depths using a pilot mounted plow as seen on the M-153 as it works to clear the passing track at Madison, located about one and one-half miles west of Westminster. The date of these photos is unknown; perhaps the blizzard of December 4-6, 1913 when the entire Denver-Boulder area was snowbound.—*Both, CRRM*

The Interurban Chronicles

A number of events within the history of the Denver & Interurban provide insights into its eighteen years of existence and relatively early demise. These events are chronicled here to give the reader a better historical perspective.

The 1916 Blizzard

On Thursday, December 14, 1916, Boulder was hit by a blizzard of uncommon proportions. Snow blanketed the area, and howling winds caused it to drift. Piling up hour after hour, it reached depths sufficient to stop Boulder streetcars and strand automobiles. In addition, the wind pulled down power lines and threateningly rattled windows in homes through the town. The Denver, Boulder & Western train from Eldora arrived two hours late that Thursday, and its run on Friday was cancelled. The engine had bucked snow drifts all the way to Boulder and more snow had fallen behind the train.

Sometime after 10:00 P.M. on the night of the fourteenth, the last scheduled D & I car from Denver fought its way past the town of Marshall. Only five miles of track separated Marshall from the D & I's Boulder depot, but on that night it was a rough five miles. It is not uncommon for winds exceeding 100 miles per hour to funnel out of the canyons near Marshall and Boulder.

The car swayed and shook in the gusts and then ground to a halt in drifting snow. It could go no further and icy grains of powder sifted through the transoms of the windows. As the interurban car continued to shake in the gusts, fear gripped the sixteen passengers on board. Marooned and worried, a few decided to proceed on foot back to Marshall. Those who tried it were blown from their feet and quickly decided to crawl back to the car. The passengers had been sitting for roughly three hours when at 1:30 A.M. a C & S switch engine arrived. It was searching for the overdue interurban. The engineer and fireman took the passengers back to Marshall in the locomotive cab. On Friday, friends drove to Marshall in automobiles to "rescue" this group. The D & I car continued on to Boulder when the C & S cleared the tracks. Within a few days the snow was cleared and everything returned to normal.

A two-car train has struggled into Globeville and paused at the start of the Tramway city line, ready to attempt the run into Denver during a heavy snow, perhaps the blizzard of December 1913.— *Edmunds Collection*

Memories

The Denver & Interurban Railroad is long gone but two Colorado railroad historians, Ed Haley and Morris Cafky, hold vivid memories of riding the Kite Route in their youth. They share their memories with the many of us who never had the experience.

The Denver & Interurban

Ed Haley

I consider myself most fortunate for having grown up in the 1920s in a family that didn't own an automobile. Thus all of our travels to and from Sunday outings had to be made by way of the trolley, the interurban or on standard and narrow gauge trains. One of our favorite locations was the resort town of Eldorado Springs. It was located in the mouth of South Boulder Canyon and we made a number of trips there via the Denver & Interurban between 1919 and 1926.

A few blocks south of our home in North Denver the Denver Tramway's route Nos. 37, 38, 81, 82, and 83 operated on West Thirty-eighth Avenue. Any car on the interurban lines (81, 82, or 83) would take you directly to the Interurban Loop in downtown Denver. Should a No. 37 or 38 trolley happen along first, you could ride them to the Tramway Loop which was just across Arapahoe Street (in the 1400 block) from the Interurban Loop. The Denver & Interurban's cars were noticeably larger than those of the Denver & Intermountain narrow and standard gauge lines which also operated through this loop.

The D & I interurbans were about the same size as a standard gauge steam train coach and were painted Pullman green. In the 1920s the cars carried the company's emblem and nickname midway on each side, just below the window sills. This logo was a dark red kite edged in gold, with the words "The Kite Route" in gold script.

There were various methods of getting to Eldorado Springs via the Denver & Interurban on a summer Sunday. The company advertised seven daily trains (even a single car was referred to as a "train") running directly through to Eldorado Springs. If you missed one of these, it was possible to take the next regular train to Boulder and transfer to the shuttle interurban which would be waiting at the junction at Marshall. The third way, and a good one to avoid, was to take a regular train to Boulder via Louisville. This route entailed a long wait at the Boulder depot before the return run back to Denver via Marshall, where a transfer was made to the shuttle.

Tickets could be purchased in advance at the office at the Interurban Loop. As I recall the Sunday excursion rate to Eldorado Springs was $1.25 with children of five to twelve going for 60¢ and this included a gate admission ticket to the resort. This type ticket had an attached stub which read "Admission Coupon—Admit One Person to Eldorado Springs Resort."

The car was entered via the rear vestibule and through a swinging door into the interior. The floor was covered by a material similar to linoleum and the comfortable seats were covered with what appeared to be soft black leather. I've been told this material is called Pantasote. The seats were reversible and we always tried to get a facing pair opposite one of the double windows. The windows opened easily and over each pair was an arched opening glazed with vertical panels of stained glass in light browns, pale greens, and opalescent white in a swirled pattern. The car interior was done in a rich, dark red wood highly varnished. The clerestory ceiling was a light green with a row of electric lights down its center. There were also some lights over the seats. One restroom at the rear served everybody.

As soon as the car left the loop and turned northeast on Arapahoe Street the conductor began collecting a city fare. I believe that during this period it was eight cents for adults and four cents for children and it would take you as far as Globeville station on North Washington Street. On reaching Twenty-third Street, the car swung northwest, passing the company shops and carbarn on the west corner of Twenty-third and Market streets, rumbling across the rickety old wooden-floored Twenty-third Street Viaduct which carried only trolleys, interurbans and pedestrians over the railroad yards and the South Platte River, coming down on Fox Street. Running north on Fox Street, the line made a long sweeping curve alongside the kilns of the Denver Sewer Pipe & Clay Company, into West Forty-sixth Avenue. The line dropped down a long hill through Globeville and made a sharp turn north onto Washington Street.

At about East Fifty-second Avenue all cars made a stop at the Globeville station and the conductor went in and signed the train register and picked up his train orders. Just after leaving Globeville station the tracks passed under a steel bridge which carried the two-foot gauge slag trains from the Globe smelter to a large slag pile on the east side of Washington Street. It was at this point that the switchover to higher AC-voltage was made. The conductor would lower the center rear vestibule window, lean out backwards, pull down on the retriever rope and lower the trolley pole, securing it under a hook on the roof. About the same time there would be a loud bump toward the front of the car as the motorman raised the pantograph with the overhead catenary, a suspended form of trolley wire different from that used over the city streets.

The Denver & Interurban's private right-of-way began at a point where the line became single track and angled northeast off Washington Street (just south of where East Fifty-fourth Avenue intersects Washington Street today), running through Retreat Park on a long curve and turning west at about where West Sixtieth Avenue would be. Shortly after crossing Washington Street, Copeland station was passed and, located on the left-hand (south) side of the single track was a semaphore. I have no idea what this signal controlled; I don't ever recall being stopped there because it was red and I believe it was the only semaphore on the line. It stood there for many years after the D & I operation ceased.

Shortly after leaving Globeville station the conductor would begin his ritual of ticket and fare collecting. If you had prepurchased your ticket, it was quite simple as all he had to do was remove the Denver to Eldorado Springs stub. However, if your destination was somewhere along the line, he had to use an Ohmer Fare Register to record the cash fare. This register was a black box about fifteen inches square and eight inches deep. It was mounted high on the bulkhead that separated the motorman's cubicle from the rest of the car. On the face of the register was a large dial with big numbers from zero to nine arranged in a circle. There were two hands mounted on the dial and pointing to the numbers. One was red, the other white. Suppose that a passenger was enroute to Standly Lake. The twenty-five cent one-way fare was registered by the conductor. He rotated a red handle and a white handle on a rod that extended from the fare register for the length of the car above the seats on the right-hand side. He would turn the red handle until the red hand on the dial reached the number two. Then the white handle was used to turn the white hand to the number five. This done, the conductor then jerked on a rope that was hung through brass loops alongside the rod. The register made a sound like an old-fashioned cash register and a small metal plate with .25 in

black on a white background would pop up in a small glass window near the top of the register and the fare was recorded.

At Utah Junction the D & I track swung in alongside the Colorado & Southern's main line north and paralleled it at a slightly lower level as far north as D & I Junction, about two miles beyond Broomfield. The ride was fast and quiet, flashing through green fields and across dusty dirt road crossings with the airhorn sounding for each and every one. At the infrequent stops to unload or pick up passengers that wonderful smell that came only from hot electric trolley or interurban motors was wafted into the warm summer air. At D & I Junction, excursion trains bound for Eldorado Springs switched onto the Colorado & Southern's branch line tracks which now carried a catenary overhead, and proceeded on west through Superior. Beyond Superior the line climbed over a ridge and dropped down a long valley through Gorham to Marshall where the train was switched to the Eldorado Springs branch. If you happened to be on a regular car to Boulder, you transferred to the branch line shuttle interurban which met all regular cars at Marshall. Eldorado Springs was just three miles to the west and ten minutes away. The beautiful mountains of the Front Range loomed just ahead and most of the passengers were shuffling picnic baskets and clothing, getting ready for their arrival in Eldorado Springs.

Summer Sundays were always busy days at Eldorado Springs. Just outside the admission gate to the resort were two long tracks paralleling a depot platform with an overhead canopy. I cannot remember any depot building. Branching from the left-hand (south) track, just east of this platform, was a track leading to the loop for turning the electric cars at Eldorado Springs. The shuttle was usually waiting on this loop for specials to arrive from Marshall. Some Sundays, when there was a large company picnic at the resort, there might be a special steam passenger train waiting on the right-hand (north) track at the platform. Catenary was strung above both tracks and the loop. The steam trains had to back out to Marshall as the loop was too tight to turn them. It was not unusual to see as many as four interurbans coupled to form a special and all of the trailers were in use on Sundays.

In those days Eldorado Springs was a first class resort with a fine hotel that had an excellent dining room. There were lots of small cottages for rent; three swimming pools filled with water from the hot springs; a dancing pavillion; picnic pavillions; the "crazy stairs" (wooden stairways with occasional covered resting platforms) that climbed high on the sheer rock walls on both sides of South Boulder Canyon. There were hiking and riding trails going in all directions. Our favorite path climbed along South Boulder Creek to Harmon Falls where we usually picnicked. Very few autos made an appearance in Edorado Springs because the roads leading to the resort were quite primitive. But it was a great place to go via the big electric interurbans. In the line's last years, after it was taken off the downtown streets, the cars operated from a special track, the farthest one out at the Denver Union Station. It was necessary to go all the way to the end of the pedestrian tunnel under the depot tracks, up the stairs to the last platform and then cross another track at a grade to reach a short concrete platform that had been added for the electrics. It was unusual to see anything but a single car waiting at Union Station. From here the relocated line went north to Utah Junction through the railroad yards—there was no more street running in Denver for the big cars.

In the 1940s I took my own family to Eldorado Springs for a week each summer. It was our good fortune to find a cottage just inside the admission gate next door to the permanent home of Mr. and Mrs. Humlong. Mr. Humlong had been the shuttle interurban's motorman between Marshall and Boulder until the line was abandoned. He had also been a motorman on the Cripple Creek District Electric lines until abandonment at which time he came to work for the Denver & Interurban. Needless to say, Mr. Humlong and I spent many an enjoyable hour looking at photos and discussing both lines.

I sincerely believe that if the Denver & Interurban had been able to survive the financial shock of its only major wreck and the era when changing over to bus operation became so popular, today it would be handling great crowds of daily commuters to and from that well-populated area to the northwest between Denver and Boulder.

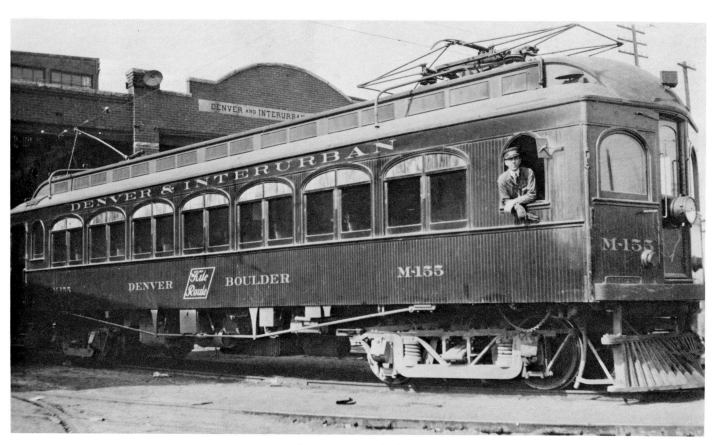

The Kite Route of Ed Haley's memories is typified by the M-155 ready to depart the shop at Twenty-third and Market streets, circa 1920. —CRRM

The Kite Route

Morris Cafky

I became acquainted with this fine electric line only in the last eighteen months or so of its existence, but saw enough of it during that period to appreciate what an excellent system of transport it was. Though I was only six and seven years of age at the time, Denver & Interurban electric trains still roll vividly through my memory.

My maternal grandmother then was living in Boulder. Our family made frequent visits to Denver, sometimes travelling from Florence via Rio Grande train, sometimes driving back up in our Buick touring car. Since my father usually had business to transact in Denver, Mother and I would journey to Boulder and stay with Grandmother. My first D & I journey started with an element of surprise. When Mother said we were to ride the interurban, I naturally thought we would leave from Denver's Interurban Loop which I had seen, and lay just across Arapahoe Street from Denver Tramway Corporation's famed Central Loop. I was a little nonplussed when Dad drove us to Union Station. I regarded Union Station as exclusively the lair of steam trains, and had never noticed electrified Track 11 when arriving there by train.

"I thought we were going to ride the interurban," I protested. "We are," Mother replied. This made no sense to me, but we walked through the pedestrian subway, climbed the stairs and emerged beneath the little umbrella shed sheltering Track 11 and, sure enough, there stood a handsome, green electric car. The car was a straight passenger motor—no baggage door—so was apparently one of the M-151—M-156 series.

We boarded and since it was a warm day—I believe the early summer of 1925—we sat down by an open window. The hour was rather early in the afternoon; I expect it was around two. Consulting the Colorado Railroad Museum's D & I's employee Timetable No. 7, effective May 31, 1925, I note that Train 313 departed from Denver at 2:00 P.M., running via Marshall. Almost without a doubt, this was the train we always rode on our Boulder-bound trips.

Presently, the car rolled smoothly out of the station, passed under the Twentieth Street Viaduct, gradually curved to the north, skirted the Twenty-third Street Viaduct and the Burlington roundhouse, then crossed the Platte River. As we were seated on the right-hand side of the car (Mother always let me sit by the window) I then noted the D & I's barn and shops and stared with great interest at this facility. Almost always, a couple of motors would have their handsome vestibules thrust out of the big doorways, and a trailer or two was usually visible.

On that first and subsequent journeys, I noticed how smoothly the big car rode as compared with city streetcars. I noticed also the comfortable, leather-upholstered seats, the fine, dark mahogany woodwork and the overhead dome lights in the car ceiling. Ahead of us a couple of paired windows was the bulkhead, dividing the smoking section from the non-smoking area where we were seated. Mother gave me to understand that ladies and children should never ride in the smoking section; that area was reserved for men smoking cigars, pipes and cigarettes, and, no doubt, telling smoking-room stories!

Another thing that impressed me on that first ride and subsequently was the speed. To me, the big car seemed to be "going like sixty." Employee timetables for D & I and C & S governing Kite Route movements specifically set maximum speed of electric trains at fifty miles an hour, and this may have been our speed. However, the powerful motors under D & I cars were certainly capable of propelling them at far higher speeds, and perhaps we exceeded the timetable maximum from time to time.

It seemed to me that the interurbans accelerated rapidly after a stop. The electric trains, of course, stopped to pick up or discharge passengers at stations such as Westminster and Broomfield, and at shelter stops situated at rode crossings. From rest, the cars would get up to speed quickly, I thought, as compared to the city streetcars and steam trains I had experienced previously.

At Westminster, a Denver-bound interurban always was waiting in the electrified passing track. On our first trip, the southbound car which must have been Train 312, had a baggage door. Since the window configuration I remember from that day corresponds to M-157 and M-158 as originally built, it must have been M-157. After the Globeville collision, M-158 was considerably changed in external appearance.

On some Boulder-bound trips, we sat on the left side of the car and I always noted with interest the paralleling C & S steam track between Utah Junction and D & I Junction. I always hoped we would meet a steam train and once we did, somewhere between Westminster and Broomfield. It was a short southbound freight, hauled, I expect, by a 600 series 2-8-0.

At Marshall, we could always see the passenger motor used on the Eldorado Springs shuttle run; Boulder itself lay just a few miles ahead. Curiously, we never did ride the electric car all the way across the university campus, down the hill, and into

Boulder's "Union Station," that elegant little stone structure which served C & S, the Union Pacific and Kite Route and had once served the narrow gauge trains of Denver, Boulder & Western.

Grandmother's house was on University Hill, three blocks west of the C.U. campus. If we had ridden all the way to the station, we then would have had to ride a streetcar back up the hill. Time could be saved by alighting at the shelter station at Baseline Road, south of the C.U. campus halt. Baseline Road then formed the southern city limits of Boulder—nothing lay to the south but vacant land. An interurban type shelter was located there, just north of Baseline Road and just west of the track.

The local cab company in Boulder evidently made a practice of sending a taxi to that point in order to pick up possible fares alighting from inbound electric trains and bound for points on "the hill." Whenever we alighted from the interurban, a taxi was sure to be waiting; we would then journey via cab to Grandmother's home.

I recall only once seeing an interurban within the city of Boulder. We sometimes journeyed downtown aboard the double-door Birney streetcars operated within the city by the Public Service Company of Colorado. This was a three-foot six-inch gauge system which once had been equipped with ancient hand-me-down cars from Denver Tramway; Birneys replaced the old-timers in the early 1920s. One day, we were aboard a Birney descending University Hill on Twelfth Street (now named Broadway, I believe). The D & I—C & S track from Marshall crossed Twelfth at grade, cut across a corner for thirty feet or so, then crossed Marine Street. The motorman of our Birney brought the car to a stop south of the crossing. A D & I whistle could be heard, sounding the customary crossing whistle. Presently a two-car, Denver-bound electric train rolled impressively over the crossing.

I remember my grandmother commenting, after the D & I train had passed, that "this is a very dangerous grade crossing." She was correct. In addition to several collisions between steam and electric trains and street vehicles, on two occasions city streetcars had collided with C & S trains. On one of these occasions, a Birney, descending the hill on a wintry day, was unable to stop on the icy rails and crashed into the side of a C & S passenger train, striking the rear Pullman.

When our visit with Grandmother ended, we seemed to take the same D & I train home, boarding at Baseline Road crossing. Again it seemed to be an early afternoon departure; Employee Timetable No. 7 would seem to indicate that we rode Train 312, departing from Boulder station at 1:30 P.M.

for Denver via Marshall.

My last ride on D & I was apparently aboard Train 312. Mother had told Grandmother that morning we must leave that afternoon; the family wanted to get home in time for me to start second grade. This would place the date in very late August or the first couple of days in September 1926. The end for D & I rail operations was just a little over three months away.

Grandmother phoned for a taxi, and the cab dropped us off at the Baseline Road shelter station. As we waited, I heard a steam locomotive whistle to the south. Around the long, right-hand curve came a northbound C & S freight train! Mother and I instinctively stepped back farther from the track as it hammered by. I distinctly recall that the headlight was mounted in the center of the big locomotive's smokebox; thus, the engine must have been one of the C & S 2-10-2s of the USRA-design 905-909 series.

The freight train passed. In a surprisingly short time, D & I 312 appeared. Colorado & Southern employee timetables issued during D & I's operating lifetime indicate that University Siding, perhaps half a mile north of Baseline Road, was electrified. I imagine that D & I 312 had gone in the hole there for the freight. Train 312 had two cars that day. The second car was one of the 200 series trailers; it had no roof-mounted pantograph. The motor was evidently well-filled for, when the train halted, a trainman put down the stool by the steps of the second car, which we boarded. I noted at once that there was one longer passenger compartment; no bulkhead and no smoking compartment. Denver & Interurban's trailers weighed little more than half as much as the motors, but the 200 rode with reasonable smoothness. We were seated on the left-hand side. As we passed the company shop just north of the Platte River, we noted a motor with trailer coupled standing outside.

We alighted under the umbrella shed serving Track 11 in Denver Union Station as we always had done. We walked toward the subway stairs and, just as we reached the head-end of the train, Mother met an old college friend. While the two ladies talked, I looked over the train. Though only as tall as the typical seven-year-old, we were far enough from the train to give me sufficient perspective to see into the front vestibule of the motor. The motorneer had left the train, but I stared with great interest at the master controller, brake valves, gauges and the motorneer's stool. I then looked with fascination at the heavy archbar trucks, electrical gear under the cars, the carbodies with their beautifully paired arch windows. All too soon, the ladies ceased talking and we headed down the stairs.

Before that year ended, the Kite Route ceased operating. Grandmother moved to Denver early in 1927 and bought a house near City Park, a stone's throw from the tracks of Denver Tramway's Route 50, East Twenty-second Avenue-Kalamath. My father was very good about taking me for streetcar rides over almost the whole of the Denver Tramway system. One day, I suggested we take an interurban ride to Boulder. Dad replied, "The interurban to Boulder no longer runs. Would you like to go up on the bus instead?

I demurred, rather emphatically!

In September 1937, I enrolled as a freshman student at the University of Colorado. The Kite Route had been gone for almost eleven years; the C & S had abandoned and dismantled its track via Marshall and the university campus during 1932. The Colorado & Southern main line now lay through Louisville.

Even as late as 1937, not many students at C.U. had their own autos; most of us were dependent on public transportation. When venturing to Denver, I usually travelled by rail. Sometimes I rode C & S Train 32, the so-called Zephyr Connection, leaving Boulder around 2:45 P.M., and sometimes Union Pacific's McKeen motor car leaving shortly thereafter. It wasn't until years later that I learned that the grey-haired, pleasant conductor on the McKeen car was C.A. Kindig, father of railfan-photographer Richard H. Kindig.

Denver & Interurban Motor Company was then operating eight scheduled trips each way between Denver and Boulder—only half the number of runs marked up by the Kite Route in the golden years prior to World War I. I rode the buses only when absolutely necessary. On one occasion, I received a salutary lesson on the relative efficiency of rail and rubber-tired transport.

The four-day Thanksgiving holiday was at hand, most students departing for their homes throughout Wednesday. Ordinarily, I would have "cut" my history class that day and taken either the C & S passenger or the U.P. McKeen car out of town. But Professor Eckardt had scheduled a particularly interesting lecture topic for that day, so I decided to catch the 4:10 P.M. D & I Motor's bus instead. When I arrived at the bus station a block west of the campus, accompanied by a friend, I got a shock. The sidewalk for half a block was jammed with prospective bus passengers. Most were students. There were a few older people; standing beside me in the crowd was Dr. Jack Ogilvie of the C.U. English Department.

We expressed the hope that more than one bus would be made available. Presently, three buses appeared. One was a new, Yellow Coach (General Motors) rear-engined vehicle. The second was a streamlined front-engine bus dating from the early 1930s, also built by Yellow Coach. The last was one of the 1925-26 Yellow Coach "Crackerboxes" which had initially replaced the electric trains. Presently, the three buses rolled off, carrying standing loads, people jammed in like sardines. A fair number of us were left behind, clutching tickets and with no transportation to show for them. The next bus would not leave until 6:45 P.M.

Professor Ogilvie softly uttered a couple of choice expletives seldom if ever heard in the chaste corridors of the Department of English. Then he told my friend and me: "Wait here. I'll see that you get to Denver."

Off he strode. His home was evidently not far away, for in five minutes the good professor was back, driving his 1930 Chevrolet coupe. Bundling us in, he drove us to the city. Very decent of him, indeed.

On the trip to Denver, it was evident that Professor Ogilvie was still most unhappy over being left behind by Denver & Interurban Motor Company. He expressed some distinctly unfavorable opinions about the bus operation's ability to handle large crowds. Then he said: "A three-car Denver & Interurban Railroad electric train would have swallowed that entire crowd, and still had room to spare!"

I thought then and still think that the Kite Route could have no more worthy epitaph.

Safety First

The growing popularity of automobiles meant an increasing grade crossing problem for the D & I. The lack of smoke which normally warned drivers of an approaching train and the high speed of the electric cars added to the likelihood of accidents. Above, a typical interurban—automobile encounter on June 22, 1916; at right Superintendent Renick examines the point of impact while another official talks with a crewman. Below is the remains of a 1924 Ford after an unscheduled meet with an interurban on October 19, 1924 at Goodview Crossing, five miles west of Louisville. The railroad eventually paid $750.00 for a settlement.—All, CRRM

THE COLORADO & SOUTHERN RAILWAY COMPANY.

F. C. VOUCHER NO. 17469

CLAIM NO. 158928   TO   The J. S. Brown & Bro. Mercantile Co DR.

MONTH OF Oct 191 3   ADDRESS   Denver, Colo. 18th & Wynkoop Sts

THE C. F. HOECKEL B. B. CO. DENVER. 1887

FOR Damage to 1 bottle Malted Milk.

Shipment covered by Denver to Boulder, Colo

WB 2522 9/17/13.

Some claims seem trivial by today's standards; $3.00 for a broken bottle of malted milk! However, there were serious accidents as when a man walking across the South Boulder Creek bridge near Eleventh Street seemingly froze at the sight of an oncoming interurban. He was struck and killed at the point where an investigator stands in this photo taken October 28, 1911.—CRRM

Trainmaster Willfong took this photo on August 29, 1924, of the remains of a truck after a grade crossing accident. In the distance a C & S freight approaches the unidentified location.—CRRM

BATTLE CREEK, MICH.

September 3, 1915.

Mr. W. F. Sterley,
Gen. Freight Passenger Agent,
Colorado & Southern Ry.,
Fort Worth, Texas.

Dear Sir:

IN RE AUTOMOBILE DAMAGED FEB. 6, 1915,
BROOMFIELD, COLORADO.

On February 6, 1915, one of our automobiles
driven by Mr. Fred L. Wright, 324 Josephine St., Denver,
Colorado, and in which was our Mr. Paul Copeland, 502
Exchange Bldg., Denver, Colorado, was struck and badly
damaged by an interurban car while the auto was crossing
its tracks at Broomfield, Colorado. A string of box
cars stood on both sides of the interurban crossing,
thus preventing the driver of the auto seeing the approaching interurban car. The interurban did not whistle
until within a short distance of the auto. The interurban was running about 25 miles an hour. The auto was in
a low gear running about 4 miles an hour.

The auto was turned completely around and knock-
ed about 20 feet, being damaged as follows:

Front of automobile smashed and top wrecked.
The following parts were destroyed,- radiator, one front
wheel, one tire, both outerface and inner tube, one front
axle, two front gas lamps, one tail lamp, front springs,
one rear fender, two radius rods, one front wheel and one
top. The following parts were damaged,- one front fender,
steering rod bent, frame rod bent.

We understand that the Colorado & Southern
Railroad own both the steam track and the interurban and
are, therefore, without question responsible for the
accident.

We realize that your department does not have
direct charge of such matters, but our Company are heavy

When a D & I train collided with a Kellogg Toasted Corn Flakes truck at a crossing in Broomfield, the railroad refused to pay any claim. The cereal company decided to put pressure on C & S officials as in this letter which continued for two pages and made very clear the message that as important shippers, better treatment was expected. On December 8, 1915, ten months after the February 6 accident, the D & I reached a settlement for the sum of $150.00.—CRRM

Aged Scout Found Dead Near Rails
Spectacular Career of "Rocky Mountain Joe" Ended —*Denver Post*

One of the strangest and saddest accidents on the Denver & Interurban took the life of one-time scout, turned pioneer photographer Joe Bevir Sturtevant. Rocky Mountain Joe as he was best known, came to Denver from Boulder to visit his son, a Grand Junction druggist, who was in town for the day. He stopped in at the *Denver Post* during the afternoon as was his custom to entertain a group of reporters with talk of the old west. About 8:00 P.M. he went with his son to the D & I ticket office in the Interurban Loop where his son purchased a ticket to Boulder but forgot to give it to his father. Joe left on the 9:00 P.M. train but when the conductor began collecting tickets he realized he had neither the ticket or enough money for a cash fare. He looked around the car for a friend since he was well known but finding none the conductor put him off at Modern, located near present day Sixtieth Avenue and Pecos Street. He stated he would walk home to Boulder, not too unusual for the old scout and a passing train a few minutes later noted him walking along the track. His son soon realized he still had the ticket, returned to the Interurban Loop and arranged for the conductor of the 11:00 P.M. train to take his ticket and pick him up if he spotted him walking. At 11:25 P.M. the train crew spotted a body along the track about one-half mile west of Modern. They found Joe dead, took his body on the train and continued to Westminster where he was placed in the station and the authorities called. When found his face was covered with blood from an apparent fall on the ballest but he had no other injuries except a broken left forearm. The Adams County coroner found no evidence of a crime and it was eventually ruled an accident. The best theory seems to be that Joe had walked a short distance and when the next train passed attempted to climb on board but fell and died apparently from the shock of the fall. At age sixty-three this was not an unreasonable possibility. Joe is seen above with his camera in his Boulder studio some years earlier. His photography covered much of the Boulder area and the mountains to the west and included the photo on the bottom of page 11. Joe was buried next to his wife in Boulder and the newspapers gave considerable coverage to the passing of this pioneer of the old west.—*DPL*

DENVER AND BOULDER CARS SMASH TOGETHER OUTSIDE CITY LIMITS

Ambulances and Fire Dept. Apparatus Are Sent to The Scene

Seven or eight persons are reported killed and two score or more injured in a head-on collision between two Denver & Interurban cars at a point about a half mile north of the Denver city limits, in Adams county, shortly before 1 o'clock Monday afternoon.

Dead are being carried to the Denver morgue and injured to the Denver county hospital and other institutions in Denver in ambulances, fire wagons, private automobiles and every other manner of conveyance which can be pressed into service.

A crowd quickly gathered to render aid and gaze at the destruction which occurred when the two trains hit. The building in the background of the panoramic view is the carriage house of the so-called "haunted house of North Washington" at 5500 Washington Street, thus pinpointing the location of the wreck.—*Photos, CRRM; Headlines,* The Denver Post

The Globeville Wreck

June 23, 1920, marked the twelfth anniversary of interurban service on the Kite route. It had run for twelve years without a serious accident, and W.H. Edmunds, was proud of that record. Following the busy Fourth of July weekend, he sent a congratulatory memo to his employees. He addressed it to "The D & I Family" and stated: "During the three day period ending July 5th, the Denver & Interurban with auxiliary service handled 16,285 passengers, being the largest three consecutive day number in its history, and this without a single accident or injury. This record is not luck, but is the result of careful, earnest and hearty cooperation and I wish to express my most sincere appreciation for such perfect team work."

Two months later, as Labor Day approached, Edmunds expected that team work to continue. Unfortunately, carelessness and fate would combine to make the holiday a sad one.

Labor Day dawned bright and sunny, but it started on the wrong foot for trainmen Fred Schulze and Lawrence Cripps.

Schulze was a veteran conductor with seventeen years of service on the Colorado & Southern, but he had rarely worked on the D & I. He was called from freight service because his seniority gave him rights to extra D & I runs. Schulze was glad to get the extra work, but felt uneasy about his lack of knowledge regarding D & I schedules. He asked for a timecard at the shops before his first run, but none were to be had. He was told to check at the Globeville Depot. Upon arriving at Globeville, he asked again, but C.H. Obland, the station agent and train order operator, had none to give out. Obland seemed unconcerned about Schulze's needs and proceeded to take care of other business. According to the rules, a conductor was not to run without a timecard, and if none was issued to him by the company, he was to hold his train until the company supplied that document. Such rules were for the protection of everyone on the line, but a man who clung to them could be very disruptive. Schedules on a fast paced passenger line could become chaotic if a train just sat while busy agents and trainmen searched out a timecard and brought it to Globeville. Schulze decided to simply trust his motorman and the dispatcher to keep his train out of schedule conflicts. He assumed the Globeville operator would notify the dispatcher of his predicament.

Lawrence Cripps, the motorman, had a timecard but did not share it, and he was not very talkative that day. He was sick and did not want to be at work. He had missed work on Sunday as a result of food poisoning, and wanted to stay in bed on Monday, too, but the dispatcher needed every available motorman to cover the Labor Day schedule. There was no one else to call, so Cripps reluctantly came to work. Cripps had been a C & S engineer for three years and a D & I motorman for

two, but he only occasionally worked. His seniority was low and he was only called when regular men were unavailable.

Fred Schulze and Lawrence Cripps were assigned to Extra 158. It was a two-car train making runs from Denver to Eldorado Springs and back. As an extra, it had no established schedule and did not appear on the timecard. It was, instead, governed by train orders and required to keep clear of all regularly scheduled trains.

All D & I trains were running at or near capacity on Labor Day. Denverites were heading for the Eldorado Springs resort in droves. Boulderites wanted to visit friends and families in Denver, and the miners in Lafayette and Louisville were looking for good times anywhere away from the mines.

Transportation throughout Denver had been in something of a state of chaos since August 1. A strike had shut down the Denver Tramway, and residents were forced to walk or drive in order to get around. In deference to the strikers, D & I service to Interurban Loop was suspended. Trains came and went from the carbarn at Twenty-third and Market instead. D & I crews handled operations in Denver in place of the striking Tramway workers.

Extra 158 left the carbarn for its first trip at 7:30 A.M. The run was uneventful except for Schulze's futile requests for a timecard. Upon arrival at Globeville, Schulze signed the train register, checked the lineup for conflicting trains, and then his extra headed north. There were no other station stops until Eldorado Springs. As the train went by Louisville Junction, the train order operator registered for Schulze in order to save time. Most crews on the D & I knew the schedules by heart, and they were generally rushed to meet the schedules. Since the crews needed to sign out almost as soon as they signed in, the operators customarily signed for them. The conductors and motormen just kept a mental note of which cars they had passed and which they had not, in order to keep their orders and schedules straight. On Labor Day, the Kite route was packed with scheduled and unscheduled trains as the dispatcher worked to keep the holiday crowds moving.

For its second trip north to Eldorado Springs, Extra 158 arrived in Globeville at 11:27. Coming up the line a few minutes behind it was a regular train, number 309 and following that was Extra 152. The two-car extra consisting of M-158 and trailer 204 was spotted in front of the crowded depot, then Schulze and Cripps went in for orders.

After receiving his orders, Schulze went to the register intending to sign in, but he found that C.H. Obland, the operator, had already done it for him. Schulze assumed that southbound train number

308 was due in Globeville at 12:30, so he made plans to meet it at Semper siding. Semper was eight miles north and Schulze planned to get there in plenty of time to let number 308 by. Since anyone with a timecard should know the schedule of number 308, Schulze's orders made no mention of its time.

Cripps knew that number 308 was due to arrive at 11:30 and just as his watch told him it was due, he heard a heavy vehicle pass on the street. He did not look up, but continued to read his orders as he sat in the busy depot. Moments later a conductor came in to register, then Cripps got up to leave. It was standard practice for conductors to get off at Globeville while their trains and the passengers continued on to the carbarn. Because of this, Cripps was not surprised when he did not find number 308 outside. Unfortunately, he also did not notice that number 309, a northbound, had just pulled in behind his train.

The fateful die was cast shortly after 11:30 when Schulze said to Cripps, "If nothing more is bothering us, we might as well go." They pulled to the end of the Washington Street double track so the brakeman could lower the trolley pole and raise the pantograph, then left. James Murphy, the brakeman, was a conscientious man, but he also had no timecard. He depended on Cripps and Schulze to keep the train in the clear.

C.H. Obland paid no attention as these men read their orders, and he was busy selling tickets when they left. He did not feel it was his job to see that they had timecards or checked the register for trains.

While Cripps accelerated out of town, Schulze worked to the front collecting tickets. As he did so, a worrisome thought kept gnawing at his mind. Could number 308 be due at 11:30? Just as he stepped into the front vestibule to ask, number 308 roared into view.

Train number 308 was four minutes late when it headed south from Boulder. It consisted of a single car and it was standing room only with travellers. There were seats on the car for 59, but after picking up miners at Louisville, the passenger count reached 136. No space remained in the aisles or in the rear vestibule, so members of the Louisville section crew rode up front with the motorman and conductor.

Robert Stevens, the motorman, struggled to make up lost time, but the M-153 was just not able to respond. Its gear ratio had been lowered for reduced current consumption, and it could barely sprint above fifty. He was six minutes late at Westminster, racing by at 11:24. It was 11:28 when he passed Dewey siding, and he raced by there too. He had orders to wait for northbound number 309 at Dewey, but was only to wait until 11:26. He was

How Monday's Wreck Occurred

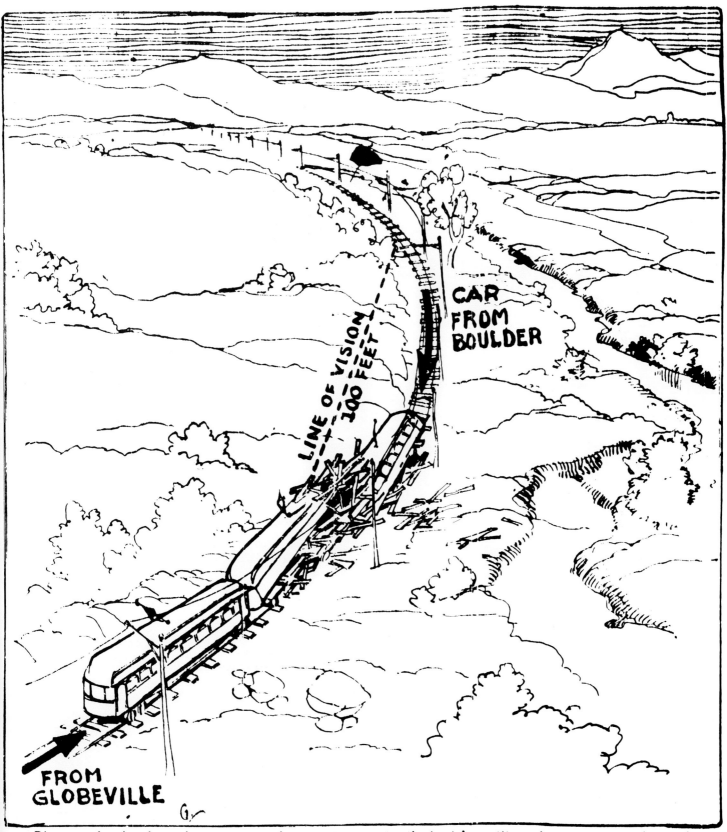

LINE OF VISION 100 FEET

CAR FROM BOULDER

FROM GLOBEVILLE

Diagram showing how the cars were obscured from each other's sight until too late to prevent the crash.

The Denver Post

to head in to Globeville if the northbound had not arrived. Stevens cut his speed to thirty-five as he rounded the outside of Retreat Park Hill. It had a one percent descending grade and crossed Fifty-fourth Street just before reaching Globeville. He was worried about automobiles or cattle which could be in his way, but instead he found Extra 158. With a closing speed of 60 miles per hour, and only 360 feet separating the trains, there was little time to react. At the most he had four seconds. Stevens threw the brakes into emergency, opened the sand valve, pulled one long blast on the whistle, and climbed up onto his window sill. He then shouted "jump," and the Louisville section hand dove out the open lefthand doorway. Jose Cortez, the section foreman, just stood there frozen by shock, but Conductor W.G. Grenamyre tried to run down the aisle to the rear of the car.

As the cars slid together on squealing wheels, there was nothing more for Stevens to do. He jumped out the window and heard the cars collide before he hit the ground.

In the on-rushing extra, Lawrence Cripps hit the brakes, then both he and Schulze jumped too.

The passengers had no warning as the two heavy trains came together. Most were thrown from their seats and eleven people in M-153 were killed almost instantly. With the impact, M-158 rode over the end sill of M-153. It demolished the front vestibule and plowed through the crowded passenger compartment. It telescoped into the interior of M-153 for a distance of fifteen feet before grinding to a halt.

A half mile south at the Globeville depot, Obland suddenly realized the extra had left town. It was 11:32 when he ran out hoping to flag it down, but he discovered he was too late. The car was already under the high voltage wires and pulling away. He and the motorman of train number 309 hoped aloud that the extra would make it safely around the hill. From there and beyond, the trains might see each other coming in time to stop. They knew their hopes were in vain when moments later, injured Brakeman James Murphy struggled into view waving his signaling flag.

Doctors, passengers and D & I crewmen all rushed to the scene to give aid. The strong helped the weak from the wreckage, then the cars were pulled apart. Although the two motor cars appeared to be total losses, the trailer, the track and the trolley wires were unscathed. By 5:00 P.M. C & S wrecking crews had the line clear.

The accident was costly, with 12 dead, 214 injured, personal injury damages totaling $145,-000.00, and two interurban cars out of service. It

was a cost which was hard to bear for a company that was barely able to pay its debts before the wreck.

Service immediately resumed, but the wreck was front page news in Denver for weeks. A coroner's inquest was held, and after hearing testimony, it convicted Schulze, Cripps and Obland of criminal negligence. All were fired. Stevens and Murphy were injured but later returned to service. Cortez and Grenamyre were among those who died in the wreck.

The Colorado Public Utilities Commission and the Interstate Commerce Commission also investigated the wreck. When the ICC published its findings, two months later, eleven major problem areas were spelled out.

1. The conductor had no time card.

2. The conductor was unfamiliar with the schedules.

3. The brakeman had no timecard.

4. The company placed these men in service without timecards.

5. The company had no timecards available.

6. The men violated the rules by operating without timecards.

7. The conductor did not check and sign the register as required by the rules.

8. The conductor did not give the motorman a written check of the register as required by the rules.

9. The Globeville operator registered for the crews, thus giving them no reason to check the register.

10. The line did not contain block signals.

11. The crew violated a rule prohibiting passing from double track to single track without ascertaining whether all superior trains which were due had arrived.

In conclusion, the ICC investigator stated that "In order to eliminate the danger of another accident of this character, prompt and efficient steps should be taken to see that the rules are enforced and obeyed by all concerned, and that employees are properly qualified and are furnished with necessary equipment before they are allowed to go on duty."

Within a few hours of the wreck, as soon as the dead and injured had been removed, the C & S wreck train was brought in through Modern Junction to the north side of the accident, pulled the cars apart and had the line open by late afternoon. Most of the deaths and serious injuries were to passengers and crew riding the Denver-bound M-153 into which the M-158 was thrust by the force of the impact, the baggage section offering its passengers some protection.— *Top, Henry Coperous Collection—Courtesy Don Robertson; Below, CRRM; Bottom, E. J. Haley Collection*

INTERURBANS CRASH OUTSIDE GLOBEVILLE

Between 10 and 12 are dead and approximately 50 injured as the result of a collision between two Interurban cars in Retreat Park, outside the city limits, on the Boulder Interurban at 1:10 o'clock.

The crash came when motor No. 153 and trailer No. 204, a special running from Denver to Eldorado Springs, collided head-on with regular train No. 308 just across the county line near the smelter in Globeville.

Albert Stevens, motorman of the outbound car, claims his car had no orders to wait at the switch further in. When he saw the crash was inevitable he leaped from the car, sustaining severe injuries.

All hospitals are being used to care for the injured.

Soldiers from a nearby post assisted in clearing away the wreckage and loading the dead and wounded into conveyances.

Every hospital in the city received victims.

DEAD:

E. N. Carveth Louisville, Colo.

Joe Chapman, 13th and Arapahoe.

William Zarina, Louisville, Colo.

Frank Dalby, 40, Louisville, Colo.

C. W. Grenemayer, conductor car 308.

L. E. Cripps, 3059 W. 29th, Denver.

Scenes at the County hospital were sickening. Overseas surgeons in attendance said, between relays, that no receiving hospital back of the trenches every witnessed a more ghastly sight.

Ambulances hurrying from the scene were jammed with mangled humanity thrust into autos in the mad effort to get them to the hospitals.

The brother of William Zarina, one of the killed, said that he, his brother and Frank Dalby were riding on the front of car 308. All jumped to avoid the crash, but William and Dalby were killed.

COMPANY STATEMENT

In an official statement soon after the accident, G. W. Richards, general agent of the Denver & Interurban railway, said:

"Motor No. 153 and trailer No. 204, running as a special from Denver to Eldorado Springs, collided with regular train No. 308 just across the county line beyond the smelter in Globeville.

"No. 153 did not wait for No 308 in Globeville, altho the latter train had the right of way.

"The conductor of 308, C. W. Grenameyer, was killed, as were a number of other passengers whose names we do not have at present.

"Both conductors on No. 153 were injured, tho not seriously. The motormen jumped and escaped with slight bruises and cuts.

"A full and complete investigation into the accident will be made to fix the responsibility.

"Coroner Jones of Adams-co, Chief of Police Armstrong and Manager of Safety rFank M. Downer are on the scene assisting in the work of caring for the injured."

Globeville Wreck Report

Less than five hours after the wreck occurred C & S Superintendent Renick dispatched this concise report to President Rice and several other officials.

MAILGRAM

Denver, September 6, 1920
4:20 PM

Gentlemen:

At 11:30 AM date at three poles north of D&I pole 27, about one-fourth mile north of Globeville, D&I passenger Ex 158 north, Conductor F.W. Schulze, Motorman L. Cripps struck D&I train 308, motor 153, Conductor W.G. Grenamyre, Motorman Al Stevens, head on. As near as we can tell at this time, D&I passenger Ex overlooked No. 308. No. 308 passed Westminster at 11:24 AM, Passenger Ex left Globeville about 11:28 AM. They signed their orders at 11:27 AM. As near as we can tell at this time Conductor Grenamyre and possibly four to seven passengers were killed and a number injured, the exact count of which have been unable to determine as the County Hospital ambulance and other ambulances together with automobiles immediately set to work rescuing the dead and injured from the wreck. In the confusion no accurate check could be made. Both trains were well loaded with passengers. The Extra carrying trailer which was well filled (sic). All of the killed and most of the injured passengers were on train 308. Cause for the few injuries on the passenger extra no doubt due to the fact that the front end of motor 158 had baggage end in front, and passengers were behind this, and in the impact cars did not telescope beyond a point about 15 feet from the front end. Latest reports show that Brakeman S.E. Crosley was perhaps fatally injured, Motorman Cripps had both legs broken, and was taken to hospital. Motorman Al Stevens cut about head and face and suffering nervous shock. Conductor Schulze suffered bad nervous shock but not otherwise injured. Conductor Grenamyre had neck broken. Brakeman Murphy on special had fractured ribs. No damage to track and no damage to trailer 204 on Ex. Estimated damage to Motor 153 $12,500.00 and No. 158 $12,500.00. Only one pair wheels derailed, and that was on 158. Balance of trucks bunched under cars but not derailed. Quite a few of the injured seriously hurt and probably some of them will die. Called the police and fire department from Denver, who cleared the ground and kept the people back after the dead and injured taken care of. Public Utilities notified, as well as Mr. Doolittle and Drs. McLaughlin and Manns. In the confusion and due to the fact that one conductor killed and the other out of his mind, it is practically impossible to get a list of the killed or injured or to fill out form 2537.

**Yours truly,
H.E. Renick**

This train order was issued to the crew of Extra 158 (as well as to the crews of Extra 152 and scheduled Train No. 309 which were following) and gave them rights over Extra 703 coming toward them as well as allowing Train No. 309 to run just five minutes behind the extra. No mention is made of any meet with Train No. 308 because it was a regular scheduled train with rights over extras. Pasco Lorenzo of Louisville was one of the luckier passengers in the wreck; his injuries were apparently minor as reflected in the statement in the amount of $11.15 from Dr. W.L. Snair for care to his injuries.—*All, CRRM*

W. L. SNAIR: M. D.

LOUISVILLE, COLORADO Oct 12 1920

Mr. Pascoe Lorenzo

Louisville

Statement rendered monthly.

12/21/20

Statement of account for Professional Services Rendered injuries received in Interurban Wreck 9/6 $11.15

(The items of this statement may be seen by calling at the office.)

FORM 19 — C. & S. FORM 1003.

THE COLORADO & SOUTHERN RY. CO.

Train Order No. 52 19

To 158 and 152 and 309

At .... STATION. X .... Opr.; 11.18 am

Motors 158 and 152 run as 2 passenger extras Globeville to Marshall on 2nd trip with right over exa 703 South Louisville Jct to Marshall. Passr exa m 158 North and no 309 may run on a 5 min block. Passr exa 158 and 152 North via Louisville Jct

The Denver & Interurban Wreck near Globeville in 1920

As told to E.J. Haley, by S.L. (Les) Logue.

In 1920 Les Logue and I lived within two blocks of each other in North Denver and played together as small boys. In later years we were closely associated as officers of the Rocky Mountain Railroad Club. A number of times I heard Les describe his experience as a passenger aboard the outbound special train involved in the head-on collision with a scheduled inbound single car just north of Globeville on Memorial Day, September 6, 1920. My recollection of Les' story of the wreck follows.

As many families did on Labor Day, Les Logue, his older brother Caddy and his mother and father decided to have one last picnic of the summer. About ten o'clock that Monday morning they rode a North Denver trolley downtown to the Tramway Loop and walked across Arapahoe Street to the Interurban Loop. In the depot they purchased roundtrip tickets on the 11:00 A.M. special for Eldorado Springs where they planned to have their picnic and relax for the rest of the day. When the two-car extra pulled into the loop, they luckily decided to ride the trailer—it would be a last ride for some of those who chose to ride the motor car.

The trip along city streets out to Globeville was uneventful and Les remembered crew members going into the small Globeville depot or office to pick up their orders. As soon as they reboarded, the train left the station and picked up speed as it veered off North Washington Street onto the Denver & Interurban's private right-of-way. Mr. Logue decided to walk up to the smoking section in the front car, stood up and without any warning and only seconds later there was a tremendous crash and Les and Caddy were hurled from their seat into the back of the seat in front of them and their father fell in the isle. Les recalled the awful sounds of splintering wood and breaking glass and the screech of metal against metal. But his most vivid recollection was of the trailer raising into the air and settling back onto its trucks and then the car filling with a choking cloud of dust which made it hard to see and breathe. There were a few seconds of absolute silence before the screams of trapped and injured passengers were heard. Some parents began calling out the names of their children from whom they had been separated.

It was some minutes before Mr. and Mrs. Logue could extricate themselves, their sons, and their belongings from the tangle of seats and climb down from the car. Les remembered retrieving their box camera which had been on the seat with him. Outside the trailer, which had stayed on the rails and was not badly damaged, pandemonium reigned. Dead and badly injured passengers were scattered about the scene and many of the injured were screaming in pain. Dazed and bleeding passengers were wandering around the wreckage looking for friends and relatives. Some passengers who had not been hurt were trying to help those still trapped in the jumbled wreckage of the two motor units which had telescoped almost halfway into each other. Since the wreck had occurred north of the city limits, it was quite some time before police and fire equipment arrived on the scene and the badly injured began to receive some care.

Of course, the Logues abandoned all plans for their picnic and had to consider getting home. Although the end of the Globeville carline was only three or four blocks south of the wreck site, Mrs. Logue was adamant—no more trolley rides for her family. She marched her husband and small sons all the way back to North Denver, lugging their picnic basket and camera. Les never forgot that almost four-mile hike on a hot afternoon, nor was he ever able to forget that his family had their old box camera fully loaded with a fresh film pack and failed to take even one picture of the wreck and the rescue efforts. He often said how he wished one member of the family would have realized history was being made that afternoon and would have made a photographic record for posterity. Les also never forgot what a long time it took to convince his mother that it was safe to ride a trolley again.

As for myself on that long ago tragic afternoon—I was spending the day at Lakeside Amusement Park with my family. I can remember that in the late afternoon newsboys were walking through the park peddling an extra paper and loudly proclaiming the disastrous wreck on the D & I near Globeville with its tragic toll of dead and injured. I'm sure my parents were shocked because Eldorado Springs easily could have been our destination on that fateful day. However, they must not have been too badly shocked as we managed to ride the line a few more times before it was abandoned.

The Globeville wreck actually occurred in an area of unincorporated Adams County just beyond the Denver city limits known as Retreat Park (see map on pages 116-117). The homes in the area were cleared some years ago as part of an urban renewal plan but little redevelopment has since taken place. The photos above and at right were taken in the spring of 1986 from the approximate location of the carriage house behind the Bomareto property at 5500 North Washington Street, better known in the area as the "Haunted House of North Washington" because of the rather ghostly look to the one-time fine home of John Hindry. The same carriage house can be seen behind the wreck in the photo on page 134 and appears left of the house in this view of the 1950s thus establishing the wreck site. The wreck took place at approximately Fifty-fifth Avenue and Ogden Street. The view above is of that intersection looking northeast with the utility pole on the right-of-way. Ogden Street is seen at right running south to an intersection with Fifty-fourth Avenue (County Road 153 on early maps) with Denver in the background.— *Below, DPL; Others, William Jones*

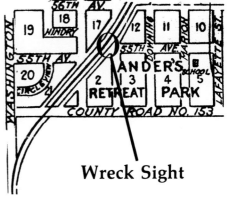

Wreck Sight

143

On an afternoon in 1925 newly delivered motor bus 22 was posed alongside M-159, itself freshly painted after rebuilding from trailer 201 with the electrical equipment from M-153 which had been destroyed in the Globeville wreck some years earlier. Decisions were already being made that would soon spell doom for the handsome green interurbans.—CRRM

6

Good Times and Bad
Receivership, Buses and Abandonment

Foreclosure and
Receivership 1918-1921

The Colorado and Southern was not in business just to run trains. The business of business is making money, and by 1918 it was apparent that the D & I was making an increasingly negative contribution to the corporate bottom line.

The subsidiary railroad which was built for $1,079,000.00 had failed to generate profits. Instead, it was rapidly accumulating debts. Overdue payments to the C & S and other creditors were already in excess of one million dollars. Due to chronic low revenues, the amount of debt kept growing. Interest on the C & S owned construction bonds was $64,740.00 per year and the D & I had made no payments since 1913. Because the D & I could not pay its operating costs, funds had been advanced by the C & S to cover them. Repayment of these funds was also overdue. The total past due debt to the Colorado & Southern was $840,828.00. Even if the C & S continued to forgive these debts, in hopes that the future would bring better days, there were other creditors whom the D & I was unable to pay. Roughly $12,000.00 was owed to ten companies ranging from the Denver Tramway to Westinghouse, $3,600.00 was owed to employee unions; and $11,000.00 to the construction bond trustee, Guaranty Trust Company. All of these creditors were prepared to sue in court for payment. An additional $42,302.00 was owed to creditors who did not threaten to sue.

The C & S sought to turn this situation around and do so quickly. To achieve profitability, the D & I would have to significantly cut costs and increase revenues. To bring this about would require concessions from both the creditors and the governmental regulators. The concessions would be hard to get unless the company's existence appeared to be at stake. Increased revenues would have to come from fare hikes which the public was sure to oppose. Cutting costs would require changing contracts and franchises which were far from expiration.

The Colorado Public Utilities Commission could not be depended upon to side with the interests of the Colorado & Southern, and neither could the local courts. In order to avoid those unpredictable arenas, the legal maneuvering would have to take place in federal court. On June 11, 1918, moves were made to give primary jurisdiction in the matter to the U.S. District Court for the District of Colorado. Guaranty Trust Company of New York filed a foreclosure suit on behalf of the bondholders. The D & I was declared to be in default on bond interest payments, thus the entire bond principal was immediately due in full. Because Guaranty Trust was an out-of-state institution, the suit was a federal matter. Since the bondholders could ask that the property of the company be liquidated to pay off the bonds, the future of the company was definitely at stake. The other creditors were faced with the potential loss of a client and the possibility that any claims they had would be paid off for a few cents on the dollar.

On June 12, 1918, William H. Edmunds was appointed receiver for the D & I. As receiver, the court granted him authority to manage the company and its assets independently from the board of directors and the company officers. Edmunds provided the court with a $75,000.00 bond, to insure that he would perform his job properly; then he went to work with vigor. He was a skilled negotiator who knew how to run a railroad, and most importantly, he fully understood that his bosses at the C & S were in business to make money.

The first order of business was to abandon the Fort Collins Street Railway. That line hung like a millstone around the D & I's neck. Its existence served no useful purpose for the company, and it generated losses in every year of operation. Still, an abandonment request would probably be blocked or delayed indefinitely by the public outcry at a PUC hearing. Within a month after his appointment, Edmunds persuaded the district court judge that the street railway had to go. At the direction of the court, he went to the PUC requesting an emergency abandonment order. This was not requested merely for the convenience of the D & I, but rather to protect the bondholders. The PUC granted the request immediately and the streetcars ceased to run. The absence of service then became a bargaining chip as Edmunds negotiated the sale of the line to the city.

In order to further improve the company

finances, Edmunds persuaded the city of Boulder to waive that part of its franchise which required sixteen trains per day between Boulder and Denver. In order to reduce operating costs, a late morning train, a mid-afternoon train and a late evening train were cut from the schedule. From 1919 on, the D & I ran thirteen trains per day. Edmunds also persuaded the district court judge to assist him in gaining electric power rate concessions from Western Light & Power Company.

Next came the issue of increasing revenues. In April 1918, the D & I had requested Interstate Commerce Commission approval for a fare increase. That request was denied, but in July, Edmunds made a second request. This one, which was made on behalf of an insolvent company struggling to get out of receivership, was approved.

Increasing ridership would also be a source of added revenues, but Edmunds saw no way of bringing this about. In 1908, the convenience of D & I service had generated new traffic. People who had seldom ridden the C & S steam trains rode the interurbans frequently. Ridership had climbed until 1911 and then it began to fall. It declined in each succeeding year except 1914. The lineside population failed to grow, but highways and automobile ownership did. Autos were already siphoning away business in 1913 when Henry Ford introduced mass production within the automobile factories. Automobile ownership on a massive scale put transit ridership into a permanent tailspin.

Declining ridership was not a problem which was unique to the Denver & Interurban. As a result of it, few interurban lines were built anywhere in the United States after 1912. The ridership crisis immediately claimed those lines which were weak, and eventually it claimed them all.

In the Denver-Boulder area, ridership on the Colorado & Southern's three times daily steam trains fell even more dramatically than that on the Kite route. The Union Pacific also had low ridership, but it was not in direct competition with the D & I. The twice daily Union Pacific trains ran a longer slower route via the towns of St. Vrains and Erie.

While traffic fell off, inflation fueled an increase in the cost of labor and materials. Between 1916 and 1920, the price of steel axles increased by 208 percent, copper wire by 97 percent, and railroad ties by 112 percent. The primary source of this inflation was the impact of World War I. Wartime deprivation, post-war prosperity, and the need to pay off the cost of running a national war machine combined to drive up wages and prices.

The United States entered the war on April 6, 1917, and fought until the armistice on November 11, 1918. More than two million men were sent to fight in France, and the federal government took control of strategic industries to marshall war production. The United States Railroad Administration was created to take control of America's railroads during this period. Among other things, it ordered both rate hikes and employee wage increases in an effort to keep the railroads on an even keel. Since the D & I carried no freight and served no areas which were not served

Noted Denver photographer L.C. McClure who had taken numerous pictures of the D & I when first opened, returned a final time in 1925 for this photo as preparations were being made for the start of bus service.—DPL

by the C & S, the USRA chose not to take it over.

USRA directives set the stage for one of Edmunds' next challenges. Effective January 1, 1918, the USRA ordered a wage increase for trainmen on railroads under its jurisdiction. The C & S implemented the ordered wage increase, but the D & I did not. D & I trainmen considered this situation to be unfair and inequitable. Most of them were ex-C & S employees who held seniority rights to jobs with both companies. They considered the two companies to be almost one and the same, and they felt the wage scales should remain equal. The unions representing motormen, conductors and brakemen took up the issue with management, and both sides agreed to go before the Railway Board of Adjustment for arbitration.

The board was not anxious to handle this case since it lacked jurisdiction over railways not controlled by the USRA. Thus it rendered a somewhat equivocal, non-binding decision. On the points of law, it agreed with the contentions of Edmunds and the C & S lawyer. It ruled that the Denver & Interurban Railroad and the Colorado & Southern Railway were not one and the same company. In addition, the D & I was now controlled by a court-appointed receiver who was directed by the court. Thus the D & I was neither directly nor indirectly under the authority of the USRA and could not be required to implement the wage increase. Legal matters aside, however, the board urged the D & I to pay the increase in the name of fairness and equity. Edmunds declined to do this and instead applied the company's revenues to paying off its debts.

By February 20, 1920, Edmunds had raised enough money to pay off all debts except the overdue bond interest. He had reduced operating costs, held wages constant, sold surplus Denver real estate, and sold the Fort Collins Street Railway. The company seemed well on its way toward solvency when it was hit by two economic bombshells. The Globeville wreck on Labor Day resulted in the payment of personal injury claims totaling $144,747.00, and the U.S. Labor Board granted a twenty-one percent pay increase to railroad employees.

Edmunds applied for a fare increase in order to generate cash to pay for injury claims, but he was rebuffed by the Interstate Commerce Commission. The ICC ruled that "patrons of a utility cannot be legally required to bear the burden caused by negligent acts of the utility and its agents. . ." Undaunted, Edmunds applied again a few months later. This time he claimed that the fare increase was to pay for higher labor costs and improvements to service. This increase was approved.

By June 1921, the only debt remaining was

$480,155.00 in accumulated overdue bond interest. The future impact of the twenty-one percent wage increase was unknown but it appeared to be manageable. On the whole, the C & S was satisfied that the Denver & Interurban was moving toward profitability. Thus, it deferred its claim to the bond interest for five years. That grace period was to end on July 1, 1926. The only condition attached was that the D & I must pay, when due, all interest accruing after July 1, 1921. The C & S formally requested that Guaranty Trust Company dismiss its foreclosure suit, and Edmunds was discharged as receiver on June 28, 1921. Control of the D & I assets was returned to its board and its officers on July 1, 1921.

The board, which was primarily made up of C & S officials, was pleased with Edmunds' performance in the role of D & I receiver. As a result, he was elevated from his old job of electrical engineer and trainmaster, to the post of general manager. Andrew Whiteford was then promoted from conductor to trainmaster.

Buses and Abandonment of Rails

Following its release from receivership, the Denver & Interurban Railroad enjoyed two good years. In 1921 and 1922 it showed a profit. Colorado & Southern officials hoped this would continue, but higher fares and lower costs were not enough to ensure the D & I's future.

As highway travel mushroomed, it became increasingly difficult to fill seats on the big green cars. Not only were people driving their own automobiles, jitney operators with touring cars were offering to do the driving for them. These one-vehicle transit companies sprang up almost overnight. They drove specific routes but offered irregular service and often cruised the streets looking for passengers. The jitney fares were low, but these companies were prone to changing routes and going out of business without notice. The existence of jitneys did not bode well for the future of rail service, but in the early 1920s, they were more of a nuisance than a competitor.

A much greater threat appeared on the scene with the arrival of the omnibus motor coach. Colorado's first intercity "bus" company received a Certificate of Convenience and Public Necessity from the Colorado Public Utilities Commission in February 1921. This was the Paradox Land & Transport Company. It established a route between Denver and Fort Collins, via Lafayette, Longmont and Berthoud. The majority of its business was between Lafayette and Denver. With five, twenty passenger, White brand buses, and fares which undercut the Colorado & Southern, it developed a very profitable operation. Business grew rapidly and the fleet was expanded to meet the demand. Fleets of buses could provide regular service to any place reached by a road, and they could modify their routes without cost. They did not require the construction or lease of private rights-of-way. Also, their labor costs were minimal. One low paid driver could do the work which required a motorman, a conductor, and a brakeman on the D & I. By the end of 1924, every sizeable city in Colorado except Boulder was served by intercity buses. Until that point in time, the Colorado & Southern had kept them away through intimidation.

The lure of potential profits, however, was strong. In 1924, several bus companies began eyeing the Denver-Boulder market and making preparations to operate that route, over the objections of the C & S. In order to forestall these ideas and also eliminate the jitney operators, the Denver & Interurban filed a suit with the Colorado Public Utilities Commission. On December 18, 1924, the D & I asked that motor carrier service be prohibited between Denver and Boulder. The grounds of this request were that the motor carriers did not have Common Carrier Certificates. Much to the displeasure of the D & I officials, their suit was denied. The PUC pointed out that although the law required such certificates for railroads, it made no mention of motor carriers. The PUC thus claimed no jurisdiction in the matter. This ruling opened the door to competitors, and in they came.

During early 1925, two bus companies entered into fierce competition with the D & I, and also with each other. The Paradox Land & Transport Company and the Boulder Bus & Taxicab Company put buses on the road. The Glacier Route also proposed to do so.

These events caused the C & S to seriously evaluate the status of its interurban railroad. During the years 1922 through 1924 ridership had continued to fall. As it did, operating costs exceeded revenues and the deferral of bond interest payments continued. Although nonpayment of interest was in violation of the settlement which released the D & I from foreclosure, the C & S management was not concerned about the issue. The people who controlled the Colorado & Southern were the same ones who controlled the D & I.

The seven member D & I board of directors included Robert Rice, who was general manager of the C & S, E.E. Whitted, who was the C & S attorney, B.F. James the C & S treasurer and J.H. Bradbury, the C & S general auditor. The executive officers of the D & I were elected by the board and for the most part these men elected themselves. Rice was the D & I president, Bradbury, the vice president and general auditor, James, the secretary-treasurer, William Edmunds, the general manager, and W.G. Weldon, the purchasing agent. This group was little interested in whether the D & I did or did not pay interest. Their objective was simply to lock up the Denver-Boulder intercity transportation market on behalf of the C & S and to find a way to make money in that market. The future of interurban service looked financially hopeless, so other options were explored. In a memo dated January 10, 1925, Robert Rice stated that, "the Denver & Interurban Railroad should be discontinued in a way which would minimize the cost and loss of business to the C & S."

Another memo outlined the choices open to the corporate management team. They could discontinue electric service and run more steam trains, but this would create no significant financial saving and generate no increase in riderships. They could replace the electric cars with gas-electrics, but that would also fail to reduce costs or increase ridership. They could discontinue the Denver & Interurban, with no replacement, but that would mean giving the business to competing bus lines. Since they did not want to give up the business in the Denver-Boulder market, there was only one choice left. They could discontinue the D & I and replace it with buses of their own.

On May 12, 1925, Rice cast his lot with buses. The Denver & Interurban Railroad was directed to start a bus line and attempt to get an exclusive franchise for service. This would effectively remove all competition from the picture. The bus line was to be put in service before any moves were made to abandon the Denver & Interurban Railroad. This was because any proposal to replace electric cars with buses would face an uncertain reception at the PUC. A proposal to run buses in addition to electric cars would be sure to gain approval.

The Colorado & Southern lobbied the commissioners regarding the public benefits which could be derived from a franchise, and that idea was well received. The commissioners became convinced that excessive competition on the Denver-Boulder route would be destructive to business and not in the public interest. Thus they proposed to call for applications and award the route to whatever company offered the best deal to the riding public.

Applications were received from Paradox Land & Transport Company, Boulder Bus & Taxicab, the Glacier Route and the Denver & Interurban Motor Company. The prime contenders were Paradox and the D & IMC. Paradox was already operating and providing good service. The D & IMC, while not yet ready to roll, presented a good case. It had solid financial backing, claimed to be affiliated with the established D & I, and offered to provide service which would be complimentary to that of the electric cars. Boulder Bus and Taxicab was too small to make a competitive proposal, and financing for the Glacier Route was in doubt. The franchise was awarded to the D & IMC on August 4, 1925. Paradox then appealed the authority of the PUC to award bus franchises. It continued to operate while waiting for the state supreme court to hear the appeal.

On December 1, 1925, the Denver & Interurban Motor Company began operation. It was wholly owned by the Colorado & Southern and established for $87,000.00. It was purposely incorporated as a separate company from the Denver & Interurban Railroad. This separate status kept the D & IMC free from the jurisdiction of the ICC, railroad taxes, and railroad labor agreements.

Denver to Boulder service was inaugurated with eight new parlor-coach type buses painted silver and gold. These were the University of Colorado school colors, and choosing them was a public relations move. Six of the 108 horsepower buses were built by Yellow Truck & Coach Company and had a seating capacity of 30. Two were built by International-Harvester and carried twenty-nine passengers. The interiors of the buses were finished in mahogany and brown leather.

The president of the D & IMC was William H. Edmunds, and under his leadership the company was a merciless and efficient competitor. Within twenty days, he ran the jitneys out of business. On December 22, 1925, Edmunds turned his attention to the Paradox Land & Transport Company. By competing with it head-to-head on all of its routes and undercutting its prices, he hoped to force it out of business. Paradox would then have to sell its equipment to the D & I at fire sale prices. In an internal memo, Edmunds noted that there was not

—*CRRM*

enough business to support two bus lines and Paradox would not be able to last very long. Paradox doggedly continued to compete until its appeal was denied by the court. Then it moved its operation elsewhere.

While working to establish a bus line, the D & I officials also worked to clear the way for the abandonment of rail service. This abandonment was quietly planned for the summer of 1926. A necessary step was to eliminate any grounds for objections from the Public Service Company. Public Service was the successor to Northern Colorado Power and would be obligated to pay off the electrification bonds if the D & I did not pay them. According to a contract, the D & I made annual installment payments which would retire the bonds on October 31, 1926. When the debt was paid, the D & I would get clear title to the electrification.

The money for an early, lump sum payoff was borrowed from the C & S. The bond debt was paid in 1925, and Public Service made no comment during the foreclosure hearings the following year.

Under the direction of Edmunds, operation of both the D & I and the D & IMC was efficient; however, on August 10, 1926 Edmunds received a warning from Robert Rice. He was instructed to be careful to keep the business of the D & I, D & IMC and the C & S separate so as not to cause problems for D & I abandonment. Edmunds immediately resigned as president of the D & IMC and made it a point to have no further official knowledge of the bus line's internal workings. That proved to be a good move. A few months later, Edmunds was questioned about apparent bid rigging on a contract to carry a large group of public school students to Eldorado Springs. The bids from the D & I and the C & S were identical, while the D & IMC underbid them by a suspiciously insignificant amount. Edmunds successfully claimed this was a coincidence and that he did not know how bids were calculated on the C & S and the D & IMC.

In order to facilitate swift abandonment of the D & I, the Colorado & Southern enlisted the aid of Guaranty Trust Company once again. The trustee filed suit against the Denver & Interurban Railroad on August 30, 1926. It cited the railroad's failure to pay any bond interest for the years 1914 through 1926. The railroad was thus in default and the full face amount of the bonds was immediately due. If the railroad was unable to pay, then the trustee requested authority to foreclose on the property of the railroad and sell it in order to pay the bondholders. Although Guaranty Trust made no effort to hide the identity of the bondholders it never mentioned them by name unless asked. Thus, in most press reports, the foreclosure took on the appearance of being purely a business move

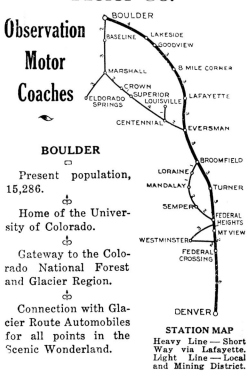

The
Denver & Interurban
Motor Co.

Observation Motor Coaches

BOULDER

Present population, 15,286.

Home of the University of Colorado.

Gateway to the Colorado National Forest and Glacier Region.

Connection with Glacier Route Automobiles for all points in the Scenic Wonderland.

STATION MAP
Heavy Line — Short Way via Lafayette. Light Line — Local and Mining District.

Special Party Service at Reduced Rates

A. W. WHITEFORD, Passenger Agent

Denver	Boulder
1715 Champa, Key. 1123	1921 12th St., Boulder 614

by a no-nonsense out-of-state financial institution.

William Edmunds was once again appointed receiver. He had pulled the line from the jaws of bankruptcy in 1921 and some observers expected him to do it again. However, his statements to the court reflected no hope. He said he did not believe that it would be possible under any conditions to cut costs or increase business materially. In addition, it would be suicidal to increase rates in an an effort to raise more money. Rates on the Denver & Interurban Railroad, the Denver & Interurban Motor Company and the Colorado & Southern Railway were very close to the same. If the D & I raised rates, it would drive business to the other lines.

Members of the public claimed the D & I's foreclosure was part of a conspiracy to take away their rail service, but they were unable to prove those claims. The city of Boulder objected to the foreclosure request noting that the D & I would have to operate until December 14, 1927 to fulfill

The Denver & Interurban Motor Co.

Denver Office
1715 Champa St.
Keystone 1123 Branch 112

W. H. EDMUNDS, V.-P. and Gen. Mgr.
C. A. WILLFONG, Supt.
A. W. WHITEFORD, Pass. Agt.

Boulder Office
1921 12th St.
Boulder 614

PARLOR COACH SERVICE

Time Schedule No. 11   Effective February 1, 1929

DENVER TO BOULDER (Via Lafayette—Short Way)

	Distance From Denver	1 Daily AM	3 Daily AM	5 Daily AM	7 Daily AM	9 Daily PM	11 Daily PM	13 Daily PM	15 Daily PM	17 Daily PM	19 Daily PM
Denver	0	8:00	9:00	10:15	11:30	1:00	2:45	4:45	5:50	8:00	11:30
Broomfield	15	8:40	9:40	10:55	12:10	1:40	3:25	5:25	6:30	8:40	12:10
Lafayette	21	8:55	9:55	11:10	12:25	1:55	3:40	5:40	6:45	8:55	12:25
Goodview	27	9:08	10:08	11:23	12:38	2:08	3:53	5:53	6:58	9:08	12:38
Lakeside	28	9:10	10:10	11:25	12:40	2:10	3:55	5:55	7:00	9:10	12:40
Boulder	32	9:20	10:20	11:35	12:50	2:20	4:05	6:05	7:10	9:20	12:50

BOULDER TO DENVER (Via Lafayette—Short Way)

	Distance From Boulder	2 Daily AM	4 Daily AM	6 Daily AM	8 Daily AM	10 Daily PM	12 Daily PM	14 Daily PM	16 Daily PM	18 Daily PM	20 Daily PM
Boulder	0	7:30	8:30	9:45	11:00	12:01	1:15	2:45	4:15	6:20	9:00
Lakeside	4	7:40	8:40	9:55	11:10	12:11	1:25	2:55	4:25	6:30	9:10
Goodview	5	7:42	8:42	9:57	11:12	12:13	1:27	2:57	4:27	6:32	9:12
Lafayette	11	7:55	8:55	10:10	11:25	12:26	1:40	3:10	4:40	6:45	9:25
Broomfield	17	8:10	9:10	10:25	11:40	12:41	1:55	3:25	4:55	7:00	9:40
Denver	32	8:50	9:50	11:05	12:20	1:20	2:35	4:05	5:35	7:40	10:20

—Intermountain Chapter, National Railway Historical Society

Flag Stops: 3850 Federal Blvd., Federal Crossing, Mt. View, Turner Corner, Eversman, Bakers, 8-Mile Corner, Lakeside.

Luxurious observation Motor Coaches used on all runs.

Special attention and rates given to Theatre Parties, Clubs, etc., for exclusive chartered Coach Service.

Denver & Interurban buses served essentially the same route as the electric cars, including Eldorado Springs, where these bathing beauties have posed to attempt giving bus riding a bit of class. It would take more than even their charm to make the bus anything but a poor substitute for the comfortable, high-speed interurbans.—CRRM

its city franchise. Boulder went on to claim that the D & I was in reality a branch of the C & S and that the C & S should continue taking care of D & I financial obligations. It also alleged that Guaranty Trust Company was merely a creature of law set up as the complainant in order to get the foreclosure suit into federal court. The towns of Louisville and Superior also joined in filing objections, but they had no franchises to enforce.

While that dispute raged in court, the Denver & Interurban Motor Company filed a request with the Public Utilities Commission. It asked authority to serve intermediate towns along the rail line between Denver and Boulder. The reason for requesting this authority was the expectation of future increases in business from these towns. The commissioners postponed consideration of the request while the railroad's case was in court.

NOTICE TO THE PUBLIC

THE DENVER & INTERURBAN RAILROAD CO.
W. H. EDMUNDS, Rec.

NOTICE TO ALL CONCERNED

By the direction of the United States Court
issued Dec. 10, 1926, the receiver of the
Denver & Interurban Railroad Co. was instructed to cease operation, effective 11:59
p. m., Dec. the 15th, 1926.

W. H. EDMUNDS, Rec.

THE DENVER & INTERURBAN RAILROAD CO.

—Rocky Mountain News, *December 16, 1926*

Otto Perry photographed these handsome interurbans on a
July day in 1927, still awaiting a call which would never
come.—*DPL*

On December 9, 1926, the district court judge ruled in favor of Guaranty Trust Company. The D & I would be ordered to cease operation on December 15. The city of Boulder's objection was rejected. According to Judge Symes, "The line had a long history of insolvency and no means of changing that. Even Boulder did not deny it. Continued operation would amount to putting Boulder's franchise claim ahead of the claims of all of the other creditors and using up the creditor's property for the convenience of the public."

The big green interurban cars were placed in storage on the yard tracks at Thirty-sixth and Fox in Denver. The shop was henceforth used only for the buses of the motor company. In a memo dated January 5, 1927, Robert Rice noted, "We used strong methods in discontinuing D & I electric service. If we furnish good service between Denver and Boulder, the feeling against us will soon subside." Edmunds was soon returned to the presidency of the D & IMC and an effort was indeed made to provide good service.

An auction of D & I property took place on February 15, 1927. It was held at the old carbarn in Denver. In order to insure that the line's dissolution was final, the property was offered up for bid in twelve separate parcels. In addition to scrappers, the bidders included the D & IMC, and the C & S, and an individual bidding under his own name in behalf of the C & S. Parcel four, all trolley overhead, and parcel five, all rolling stock, were sold to Denver Metal & Machinery Company. Parcel nine, the new shop at Thirty-sixth and Fox was sold to the D & IMC, parcel eleven, the old carbarn was sold to the C & S. When all parcels were sold, a total of $88,850.00 was raised. It was applied to the $1,079,000.00 bond debt owed to the Colorado & Southern.

The city of Boulder filed an appeal to the Denver & Interurban Railroad foreclosure decree. It reached the court in March 1927, but was ruled moot and denied. The appeal judge stated, "The city gains nothing in an appeal unless service is restored and since that is impossible, the case is moot. The railroad no longer owns the property, the trustee never had the property and the receiver ceased to have it."

When the PUC got around to considering the franchise expansion request submitted by the Denver & Interurban Motor Company, the railroad was gone. The commissioners approved the request to serve additional towns, but they also attached new conditions to the franchise. The C & S was prohibited from selling the company for ten years. In addition, if it lost money, the C & S would have to subsidize it to a minimum of $250,000.00.

The Colorado & Southern continued to manage its subsidiary bus line for two years. It then decided to exit from the bus business and concentrate on railroading. While the C & S continued to own the D & IMC, it gave Rocky Mountain Motor Company a contract to manage it. Rocky Mountain also controlled Colorado Motor Way, Gray Line and Yellow Cab in Denver. The Denver & Interurban Motor Company was operated under contract from March 1, 1929 to October 1, 1942. On that date, the C & S sold its bus line to the Burlington Transportation Company, and it became a part of Burlington Trailways. In 1946, the rights to operate between Denver and Boulder were purchased by I.B. James, a Burlington Trailways official. He organized the Denver-Boulder Bus Company, which he and his son Don James managed. In 1975, the route was purchased from them by the Regional Transportation District. RTD, which is known as "The Ride," operates all public transit services in the Denver metropolitan area. The Denver-Boulder bus route is essentially a suburban commuter operation.

The Colorado & Southern still operates through Denver and Boulder, but its line is now freight only and the population centers have moved far away from trackside. Even the C & S name is fading for the railroad ceased to exist as a separate company on January 1, 1982 upon being absorbed into the Burlington Northern Railroad.

Only two pieces of D & I rolling stock saw service after abandonment, trailers 202 and 203 which were sold to Hamilton & Gleason Construction Company in Michigan. They are seen some years later at Petersburg, Michigan on the Toledo & Detroit Railway.—*Ed Haley Collection*

With the end of D & I service the C & S had little reason to retain two lines to Boulder and in 1932 abandoned the segment from Boulder to the mines between Marshall and Superior. The rails are being removed from the university campus and soon almost all traces of the line would be gone.—*UCWH*

The shop at 3625 Fox Street was used by Denver & Interurban Motorway for a short time but eventually sold. Its last use was by the Quick-Way Truck Shovel Company which was preparing to move when Dick Kindig took this photo just prior to the building being razed for the Valley Highway's construction. The D & I's platform and Track 11 at Union Station were little used in later years. The track was weed-grown by this 1975 photo and in 1986 the platform and trackage were completely removed in preparation for redevelopment west of Union Station.—*Noel Holley*

ROSTER OF BUSES
DENVER AND INTERURBAN MOTOR COMPANY

ORIGINAL NUMBER	1930 NUMBER	DATE DELIVERED	TRADE NAME	MODEL	NO. OF CYLINDERS	BODY TYPE	SEATING CAPACITY	MOTOR NO.	SERIAL NO.	COST
* 21	821	11-1925	Yellow	Y	6	Parlor	30	30761	5096	$10,624.79
22	822	11-1925	Yellow	Y	6	Parlor	30	30749	5089	10,624.79
23	823	11-1925	Yellow	Y	6	Parlor	30	30743	5090	10,624,79
24	824	11-1925	Yellow	Y	6	Parlor	30	30734	5095	10,624.79
25	825	5-1926	Yellow	Y	6	Parlor	30	30945	5182	10,422.40
26	826	5-1926	Yellow	Y	6	Parlor	30	30960	5183	10,422.40
27	827	6-1926	International	CH	6	Parlor	29	86235	BQ962	10,517.14
28	828	7-1926	International	CH	6	Parlor	29	86286	BQ964	10,517.14
101	801	7-1927	Yellow	X	6	Parlor	21	23846	12703	7,080.91
102	802	1927	Yellow	X	6	Parlor	21	23806	12708	7,080.91
**103	803	1-1928	Yellow	X	6	Parlor	21	23081	12599	2,950.00
	829	1-1936	Yellow/GM	VT845		Parlor	29	?	?	12,200.00
	830	1-1936	Yellow/GM	VT845		Parlor	29	?	?	12,200.00
	831	1937	Yellow/GM	742		Parlor	36	?	?	?
	832	1938	White	7788		Parlor	37	?	?	?

*#821 wrecked 11-3-29 and retired 2-18-30
**#803 purchased from Colorado Springs and Interurban Railway Company 1-9-28 with 45,000 miles.
NOTE 1: Nos. 20–28 were 28'7" long, 7'8" wide.

By the time this photo was taken of bus 829 picking up passengers in Boulder during the late 1930s, the D & I was only a memory.— *Noel T. Holley Collection*

Bus 829 is seen in Denver when new in 1936. Prior to this time W.H. Edmunds and several of his associates had attempted to purchase the line but instead it was sold in 1942 to Burlington Trailways. Both Burlington Trailways and the Colorado & Southern were subsidiaries of the Burlington Railroad.

Denver & Interurban Motor Company bus 832 was purchased in 1938, the last obtained before the sale of the company to Burlington Trailways. It waits in the Denver Union Bus Terminal at 501 17th Street, a location so cramped that a turntable was built to enable buses to be turned. It is visible near the alley on the right of the photo. After World War II, Burlington Trailways sold the line and it became the Denver-Boulder Bus Company which was finally purchased by the Regional Transportation District (RTD) in 1975.—*Above, CRRM; Below, Kenton Forrest Collection*

Bibliography

The Boulder Daily Camera. Blizzard articles beginning December 14, 1916.

Bus Transportation. "Paradox Land & Transport Company," p. 221, May 1925.

Electric Railway Journal. "Catenary Trolley Construction," p. 595, September 5, 1908.

Electric Railway Journal. "Interurbans of Colorado. The Denver & Interurban 11,000-Volt Railroad." p. 509, October 2, 1909.

Electric Railway Journal. "Motor and Trailer Trucks for the Denver & Interurban Railroad Company," p. 759, October 3, 1908.

Peyton, Ernest S. and Moorman, R.A. "Denver & Interurban Fort Collins Division," *Pacific Railway Journal,* June 1957.

Swett, Ira L., *Denver & Interurban.* Interurbans Press, 1947.

Wagner, F. Hol, Jr., *The Colorado Road,* Intermountain Chapter, N.R.H.S., 1970.

Source of Information

Most of the information used in writing the text of this book was found by personally researching the extensive collection of Denver & Interurban Company records which have been preserved for historical purposes. The majority of the material was donated to the Colorado State Historical Society by the Burlington Northern Railroad. It is part of the Colorado & Southern collection. These Denver & Interurban files include letters, internal memos, authorization for expenditure records, maps and drawings. They cover both the railway and the motor company. A smaller collection of material was donated to the Colorado Railroad Museum. Some of it duplicates material contained in the files at the State Historical Society, however, documents relating to the Globeville Wreck are found only at the museum. Additional company records are located at the Federal Records Center in Denver. These consist of all documents filed with the U.S. District Court, in conjunction with suits to foreclose on the assets of the Denver & Interurban Railway. They are filed under *Guaranty Trust Company of New York v. Denver & Interurban Railway,* 1918 C.A. 6822 and 1926 C.A. 8244.

Index